William John Norbray Liddall

The Place Names of Fife and Kinross

William John Norbray Liddall

The Place Names of Fife and Kinross

ISBN/EAN: 9783337078508

Printed in Europe, USA, Canada, Australia, Japan

Cover: Foto ©ninafisch / pixelio.de

More available books at **www.hansebooks.com**

THE

PLACE NAMES

OF

FIFE AND KINROSS

BY

W. J. N. LIDDALL

M.A. EDIN., LL.A. LOND., ADVOCATE

EDINBURGH

WILLIAM GREEN & SONS

1896

TO

Æ. J. G. MACKAY, M.A., LL.D., Advocate,

SHERIFF OF FIFE AND KINROSS,

AN ACCOMPLISHED WORKER IN THE FIELD

OF HISTORICAL RESEARCH.

INTRODUCTION

THE following work has two objects in view. The first is to enable the general reader to acquire a knowledge of the significance of the names of places around him—names he is daily using. A greater interest is popularly taken in this subject than is apt to be supposed, and excellent proof of this is afforded by the existence of the strange corruptions which place names are wont to assume by reason of the effort on the part of people to give some meaning to words otherwise unintelligible to them. The other object of the book is to place the results of the writer's research at the disposal of students of the same subject, or of those sciences, such as history, to which it may be auxiliary.

The indisputable conclusion to which an analysis of Fife—and Kinross for this purpose may be considered a part of Fife—place names conducts is, that the nomenclature of the county may be described as purely of Goidelic origin, that is to say, as belonging to the Irish branch of the Celtic dialects, and as perfectly free from Brythonic admixture. There are a few names of Teutonic origin, but these are, so to speak, *accidental* to the topography of Fife. To put it briefly, in the interpretation of the place names of Fife the district may be treated as if it belonged to ancient Ireland. While this is true, there are two advantages which the student of Irish place names

possesses over the student of those of Fife : (1) In many
parts of Ireland the names are still spoken by people
using the original Celtic dialect, and (2) Even where this
is not so, they are still preserved in literary and accurate
form.   For these reasons it is almost always possible with
regard to Irish names to determine with certainty whether,
for example, Kil- stands for the Celtic *coille* = a wood, or
for a loan-word representing the Latin *cella* in the sense
of a church.   In Fife, on the other hand, the solution of
such a case depends entirely on probability.   But Fife has
at least one counterbalancing advantage.   There the
Celtic dialect ceased to be spoken, and the names in con-
sequence were stereotyped, at a period when the language
existed in a much purer form and one less weakened by
phonetic decay.   The following is a simple illustration of
what is meant.   The Fife name Beath (or Beith as it is
written in Ayrshire) is the ancient Gaelic word *beith* = birch
tree.   In modern Gaelic the final " th " of *beith* is quiescent,
and hence in the English spelling of Irish names the term
appears as -bay (*e.g.* in Ballybay).   So again the Fife
river name Leven, from *leamhan* = an elm, appears in
Ireland in English form as Laune, a name which would
have been difficult to trace to its origin had not its literary
form been preserved in Irish.

The vowel changes, moreover, indicative of Celtic inflexion, are often preserved with remarkable fidelity in the
earlier spellings of Fife names.[1]   Thus in Ardrois (now
written Ardros), *rois* is an approximation to the correct
genitive of *ros.*   The phonetic spelling of the form appears
in Portrush.   So again in Burnturk, -turk represents
tuirc, the genitive of torc ; and in Drumnagoil, *goil* re-

[1] In reference to the Gaelic entries in the *Book of Deir*, Mr. Whitley
Stokes says : " The declensional forms are scanty, but sufficient to show that
the Highlanders declined their noun in the eleventh century as fully as the
Irish."—*Goidelica*, p. 113.

presents the genitive of gall. Although there is no convenient name in English for this process of forming inflexions, it is illustrated by such formations as *feet* from *foot*.

A considerable proportion of Fife place names is thus capable of interpretation at sight, but a large number, comprising often names of the greatest interest, are to be solved only by patient searching for the earliest recorded forms, and by a careful comparative study of names similarly constructed existing elsewhere. The work is no doubt laborious, but the results are always interesting and often important. Take, for instance, the name Blebo; it is traced through Blabo, Blathbolg, till it is identified in origin, if not in locality, with the Blatum Bolgion of the Antonine Itinerary; and as this Blatum Bolgion is supposed to have been in Dumfriesshire, the inference arises that the cycles of Celtic legend repeated themselves in various and widely-separated localities. Or, take the Latin-looking word Ledlation. How easily it is read when it is found (and it is only once that it is found) written Ladglaschun. So, also, how hopeless is the explanation of Lizziewells till it is found written Latishoill; or the name Demons, unless the older spelling Demungis, and the parallel name Le Dymmyns in Cornwall, are noticed. Again, Rires would be hopeless of solution unless the old spelling Rerays, the parallel names Rywrayis, Bulwrayis in Renfrewshire, the Icelandic word *nacpnarcitr*, and the term still used in Fife to indicate a cattle-court, were all studied comparatively. Nor would it be readily guessed that the name Chemises consisted of two old French words signifying the chief manor-house of an estate. Other strange disguises are Cotton, Bungs, Goatmilk, and Nakedfield. Thus the work calls for an accurate knowledge of the rules which have been ascertained by the science of Comparative Philology to apply with inflexible certainty to the processes of phonetic degeneration. And it is not merely the comparatively mechanical process of decay due to the unconscious effort for ease of pronunciation that has to be considered, but also the subtle mental tendency to *rationalise*, by which I mean to twist a name of unintelligible meaning into a known word. And so definitely may this comparative study be carried out, that the ancient form of a place name may be reconstructed just as accurately as the zoologist will rebuild the skeleton of some extinct animal from the information supplied by a single bone.

Many are the results obtainable from the study of place names. Thus, for example, taking the names contained in this book, we find the early appearance of the country clearly set forth.

There existed a great number of peat bogs—especially in the eastern parts—which agricultural improvement has now removed. The land was generally wet and undrained, and morasses and marshy lochs were so abundant, that when a specially dry piece of land existed, its exceptional character is found to merit notice in its name (*e.g.* Strathtyrum). Forests and innumerable woods covered the country, as Fothreve, Fothros, and the many " Kils " attest. These woods consisted of oak, elm, sloe, yew, ash, birch, alder, and thorn. Bridges are not mentioned, but fords are. Tillage we find to have prevailed to a very limited extent merely, as the only words in reference are Lochornie, the barley loch, and Craigen Gaw, the winnowing rock. Yet there were rich bits of fine pasture as the Fods, Foothies, and Inches indicate. The Fife farmer of those days was pastoral, owning abundance of cattle, sheep, goats, and swine, and occasionally horses, but the modern agriculturist, with his artificial manures and his patent reaping and binding machines, had no prototype among the ancient Fife folk.

Among workmen, the skilled artificer, the smith, the shepherd, the tanner, the fuller, and the shoemaker, were known ; while the fisher, the hunter, and the athlete who could make a record throw, were duly recognised.

The list of animals comprehends the roe deer, the hind, the fox, the wild cat, the boar, the badger, and the rabbit. The eagle had his ridge and the hawk his crag, and the duck, goose, grouse, pigeon, and blackbird all give name to places ; while Thomanean and Kilnynane were respectively the knoll and the wood where the little songsters poured forth their lays. Turning to social organisation, the many names containing *baile* show that in Fife the townland system was as well developed as in Ireland, while the name Blawhidder, or town of the cottar club, proves the early existence of co-operation. The commonty was a well-established institution. The necessity for, and the means of defence are illustrated by the innumerable Duns and Cars and Raths, yet a Saxon, a Welshman, and a stranger were allowed to have settlements, and a fort of robbers and at least two towns of thieves had to be endured. Spears, arrows, and swords are referred to. The name " Knokmadyr," or " hill of the mead cup," is the only evidence of drinking customs. As illustrative of superstitions, we meet with a Fairy Glen and an old Druid or Magician's Ridge, and both a fort and a wood took name from charmed serpents. Names containing various words for pillar-stones exist in great plenty over the whole district, and the giving of these names tends to make the inference probable that these stones were erected by a race who occupied the country before the Celts. Not the least interesting of these names is the obsolete one " Mawcloych," which must have referred to the still " Standing Stones " of Orwell. The name has gone, but the stones remain.

One of the most noteworthy results of an examination

of Fife place names is the fact that therein are preserved so many of the personal names common to the cycles of Celtic legend and poetry. Thus Conchobhar or Connor appears in Balgonar; Marcan, or, in its Welsh form, Meirchion, in Markinch and Pitconmark; Nechtan, or its Welsh form, Neithon, in Naughton and in Bannaty; the sons of Calaten in Kirkcaldy; an element of Cymbeline in Beley; Breasel in Donibristle and Carspersell, Cairbre in Carberry, and so forth. Arthurian localities are represented by Craigarter, Clocharthaw, Benarty Hill, and the Maidens' Castle.

The last matter to which I shall draw attention is the comparative rarity of names of Celtic origin indicating the existence of the Christian religion. *Eagluis* = a church, occurs a few times, and the name of priest (sagart = sacerdos) and of clergy once or twice. All the Fife names beginning in Kil-, with the exception of Kilminning, are derived from *coille*, a wood, and not from the Latin *cella*, a church. The Brythonic term for a church occurs thrice, namely, in Lindores, Landifferone, and Lumphinans, and shows the existence of Welsh missionary effort. The ecclesiastical terms Dysart and Skryne are found. Nor must the special words Bantuscall and Pettuscall, signifying respectively the town and the portion of the Gospel, be omitted from notice. The saints' names to be found are those of Columba, Kenneth, Ethernan, Brotus, Finan, Nidan, Monan, Drostan, Malie, Martin, and Muirn.

With these general remarks by way of illustration the book is now left to the reader, in the hope that the results which it embodies may be interesting and useful.

ABBREVIATIONS

FOR AUTHORITIES REFERRED TO

(A) Chartulary of St. Andrews.

(B) Bleau's *Atlas*.

(D) Chartulary of Dunfermline.

(K) Skene's *Chronicles of the Picts and the Scots*.

(MS) Manuscripts in Advocate's Library.

(R) Robertson's *Index of Missing Charters*.

(S) *Register of the Great Seal*.

(T) Thomson's *Retours*.

(W) Skene's *Ancient Books of Wales*.

I. indicates a wholly or partly parallel Irish name.

The writer is under deep obligation to Sheriff Mackay for valuable suggestions generously afforded to him during the preparation of the book, and to Mr. W. Cuninghame Steele, M.A., LL.B., advocate, for kind assistance in revision.

PLACE NAMES OF FIFE AND KINROSS

Abbotshall. A hall or residence of the Abbot (in this case of Dunfermline).

Abden (of Kinghorn). Lands belonging to an Abbacy (of Dunfermline). Abdaine is a Celtic formation meaning " Abbey Lands."

Abdie. *Ebadyn.* Lands belonging to an Abbacy (of Lindores).

Aberdolloche, Aberdolo. Aber + dubh + loch = mouth of the dark loch, the river being named from the loch from which it issued.

Aberdour. Aber + dobhar = mouth of the water.

Abernethy. *Apurnethige.* Aber + Nechtan = mouth of the river bearing the same name as King Nechtan. See Naughton.

Abusuie ("*alias* Glasslie"). This appears to have been the name of lands near Kirkcaldy, and I think the name is derived from Abbacy (of Dunfermline).

Adthangy. Ath + teanga = ford of the tongue (of land).

Airbow Point. Ard + bogha = height of the bend. See Cambo.

Airdit. *Ardath.* Ard + ath = height of the ford.

Airdrie. Ard + reidh = high plain.

Aithernie. Named after St. Ethernan.

Aldendeich. Allt + cach = burn of the horses.

Aldie. Allt = burn.

Almerie cruick. " Pratum eleemosiniauratus." Cruick is a piece of land enclosed in the winding of a river.

" Almerie " indicates that it was devoted to charitable purposes.

Aly (a small stream).   Cp. the old Irish river name Ealla or Allo.

Annacroich.   *Altnacroich.*   Allt + croich = burn of the gallows.   This place is in Kinross, but Auldincroich is an obsolete name in the east of Fife.

Anstruther.   *Athernynstruther.*   *Atherne Struther* (MS). The name Uther Uchter Struther also occurs (MS). There seem to have been several "Struthers" derived from sruthair, meaning a place abounding in streams. The first part of the word may be Teutonic *andar*, meaning the other or second.

Ardros.   *Ardrois.*   Ard + ros = height of the promontory. The spelling Ardrois shows the preservation of the umlaut of the genitive, as still appears phonetically in Portrush.

Ardynnie, Ardeny.   Cp. Mons Arduenna of Cæsar, now the Ardennes.   Ard = high.

Arindinage.   Cp. Arnage in Aberdeen.

Arity Den.   *Arraty, Arachty.*   Cp. Inverarity in Forfar ; also the Irish name Arrachtain, yielding the family name O'h-Arrachtain, Englished Harrington.

Arlary.   *Ardlory, Mawardlary* (S), *Macherderrly.*   Ard + larach = height of the foundation or of the ruin. Maw is mach = field.   See Mawcloich, etc.   "Larach" is philologically identical with the English word " floor."

Arlasche, Anderlasche.

Arlick Hill.   Ard + leac = height of the stone.

Arncroach.   Ard + cruach = height of the stack (*i.e.* hill like a stack).   Cp. Bencruachan ; I. Croaghan.

Arndean.   Ard + dion = height of the place of protection.

Arngask.   *Arringrosk.*   Ard + crask = height of the pass. Drumcreesk is a name in this district in (B).

Arnot.   Ard + cnoc = high hill.   The high ground near Arnot Tower is still termed the Knock of Arnot.

Arnydie.   See Nydie.

Ashes.   Cp. Foodieash.

Auchendownie.   Achadh + dunan = field of the little fort.

Auchentrail. Achadh + rail = oak field.

Auchintelketye. (R.) Achadh + a derivative of sealg = field of the hunter.

Auchmuir. *Admore, Athmore.* Ath + mor = great ford.

Auchmuty. *Admulty.* Ath + molt (pl. muilt) = ford of wethers. I. Annamult.

Auchtenny. *Auchtevenny.* Achadh + taobh + canagh = field by the side of the marsh.

Auchterderran. Uachdar + daire = height of the oak-wood.

Auchtermairnie. *Uchtirmerny.* Uachdar + magh + airne = height of the field of sloes.

Auchtermonzie. *Auchtermunzie* (now Monzie). Uachdar + muing = height of the sedges.

Auchtermuchty. Uachdar + muc = boars' height.

Auchtertool. *Auchtertuil.* Uachdar + tuil = height of the river Tiel. Invertiel is at the mouth of this river, and the form Invirtule occurs. Tiel is derived from tuil = torrent. Cp. the Irish river name Deel.

Backevan. This old name appears to be an earlier form of Buckhaven (*q.v.*)

Baincraig. Baile + carraig = house of the rock.

Balado. *Ballatho.* Baile + ath + co = town of the ford of the yew. In Blaeu's Atlas it is given Balgadow. If this were a true form the name would mean town of thieves. But Blaeu's maps cannot be depended on when there is no MS corroboration.

Balass. Baile + eas = town of the waterfall.

Balbarton. *Balbretane.* Baile + breatun = town of the Britons, *i.e.* the Welsh. Cp. Dumbarton, *Dunbretane*, and Balbrethan in Ayr. The fact that " r " is a semi-vowel explains the variations Balbarton and Balbretane. The same change is shown in Scots " gyrs " for grass, or in Gr. κάρτος for κράτος, while in Sansk. it is formulated into a stiff grammatical rule.

Balbeadie. Baile + beith = town of birch trees.

Balbeiggy. Baile + beagan = town of the small man.

Balbeildie.

Balbeuchlie. Baile + buigleagh = town of bogland.

Balbie. Baile + beinn = town on the hill.

Balbirnie. *Balebrenin, Balbrenny* = town of Brennan. Cp. a similar ancient French name Brennacum, which is now Berny-Rivière.

Balbougie. Baile + buige = town of dampness.

Balbuthie. Baile + bothan = town of the huts.

Balcanquhal.. *Balcancoll.* Baile + ceann + coille = town at the head of the wood.

Balcarres. *Balkeros, Balcarrowis.* An English pl. Baile + carrach = rough town. Balcirrowy, a name in (S), seems to be a variant of this name.

Balcaskie = town of [M']Caskie. Cp. Kilcaskan, a parish in Ireland.

Balchristie. *Balechristin* = Christian's town, a Danish name.

Balclavie (near Elie). Baile + claidheamh = town of the sword. See Bucklyvie.

Balclerache. Baile + cleireach = town of the clergy. I. Balclery.

Balclune. Baile + cluain = meadow town.

Balcomie. *Balcolmy.* Baile + colum = town of the doves.

Balconzie. *Balquhinzie.* Consideration of this name along with the name Gartwhinzean points to a personal name Congan. The vowel change is exactly illustrated by the Irish name Drumquin = Drum + con. An original "g" after "n" is very generally written "z."

Balcormo. Baile + Cormac = Cormac's town.

Balcurvie. *Balcruvie.* Baile + craobh = town of trees.

Balcuty-(myre). Baile + ciad = town of the wood. Cp. Ballecuthe in Ross and the Cornish name Balcoath ; and for explanation, see Coates.

Baldastard. *Balstardert* (MS). Baile + sturr + ard = town of the point of the height.

Baldinnie. *Baldinye.* Baile + daingean = town of the fortress.

Baldutho. Baile + Duthac = Duthac's town.

Balekerin, Balcherin. Baile + Ciaran = town of Ciaran, literally little dark man. See Blinkeerie.

Balfarg. *Balquharig.* Baile + carrach = rocky town. The corruption of "ch" to "f" is common both in Gaelic and in English.

Balfour. Baile + fuar = cold town.

Balgallyn. Baile + gallan = town of the pillar stones. I identify it with the present Boglilie. See Rumgally. Cp. I. Drumgallan.

Balgarvie. Baile + garbh = rough town.

Balgeddie. *Balgadie.* Baile + gaduiche = town of thieves. Cp. Pitgeddie ; I. Balgaddy.

Balgonar. *Bagonawar, Balgonware, Balgonquhare.* Baile Conchobar = the town of Conchobar ; Latinised Conquovarus. Conchobar is the original form of Connor ; so Balgonar = Connor's town.

Balgonie. *Balgownie.* Baile + gamhainn = town of stirks or year old cattle. Gamhainn must literally mean one winter old (derived from "gamh," for which see Balgove).

Balgothrie. Baile + gaothrach = windy town.

Balgove. Baile + gamh = town of the wintry storm. Gamh is the etymological equivalent of Lat. hiems, Gr. χειμών, Sansk. hima, as in Himalayas.

Balgownie. See Balgonie, another place-name in Fife of the same origin.

Balgreigie. Baile + graigheach = town abounding in herds.

Balgrummo. Baile + gruamach = the gloomy town.

Balhelvie = town of [M']Kelvie.

Balhouffie. This is identical with the old name Balulphy. Baile + Ulfa = town of Ulfa, a son of Cruithne (K).

Balhousie. *Balcolsy.* In such collocations "w" stands for original "ch." Colzie is still a name near Auchtermuchty, and doubtless of the same origin as the latter part of Balhousie.

Balhucca. Baile + Acca = town of Acca. Acca was bishop of Hexham, but was driven from his see in the year 732. Skene's view is that he then founded St. Andrews, and that this was the historical basis of the legendary foundation by St. Regulus. See *Proc. Scot. Ant. Soc.*, vol. iv. p. 315.

Balkaithly. Town of Cathlach, one of the many names

in Celtic derived from cath = battle, or in Gaulish catu, *e.g.* Caturiges.

Balleave. *Ballaif.* Cp. the Irish name Balief, which is Baile + aodh = Hugh's town. The corruption of "dh" and "gh" into "f" occurs in Celtic place-names, and the pronunciation of the English word "laugh" illustrates the same phonetic change.

Ballenkirk. Baile + cearc = grouse town. I. Coolkirky. *Cearc* is literally hen, and stands for cearc fhraoich = heather hen.

Ballibevo (MS). Described as in the parish of Leslie (not to be confounded with Blebo). In (T) it is given Ballilevo or Ballilero.

Ballinbreich. Baile + breac = town of the trout.

Ballindard. Baile + dart = town of the heifer.

Ballindean. Baile + dion = town of the place of shelter.

Ballinderran. See Bandirran.

Ballingall. Baile + gall = the strangers' town.

Ballingry. *Ballingaric.* Baile + garadh = town of the garden. The beautiful situation of the lands on the south-eastern slope of Benarty Hill are aptly described by the Celtic name. The local pronunciation is Bingry, for which see note on Banbeath. I. Ballingary.

Ballintagart. Baile + sagart = priests' town. Sagart is a loan-word from Lat. sacerdos.

Ballone. *Balloun.* Baile + uan = town of lambs.

Balmadethin.

Balmain. Baile + meadhon = middletown. I. Kilmaine.

Balmakein. *Balmalkyn.* Maelcon's town.

Balmblae. Baile + blath = town of flowers. I. Ballyblagh.

Balmeadowside. *Balmaddyside.* Baile + madadh = town of dogs.

Balmerino. Baile + Merinach = Merinach's town; Merinach was the name of a companion of St. Regulus of St. Andrews.

Balmonth. Baile + monadh = town of the mound.

Balmule. *Balnamule.* Baile + maol = town on the bare rock. Balmolan is a name in (A), but it is uncertain if identical with Balmule.

Balmullo. Baile + mullach = town on the summit.

Balmungo. Baile + muingeach = town of sedges. Cp Pitmunzies.

Balmuto. *Balmutach, Balmulto.* Baile + molt (pl. mult, = town of wethers. The Teutonic equivalent occurs also in Fife, viz. Weddersbie. " Molt " is the origin of the English word " mutton," through O. F. moton, Low Lat. multo.

Balnacarron. Baile + carran = town of the rocky land. I. Carran.

Balneil = Neil's town.

Balnethil. Baile + coille = town of the wood.

Baloyngy = town of Oingus or Angus.

Balquhomry. Baile + comar = town of the confluence of two streams.

Balram. *Balrahame.* Baile + rathan = town of the little fort. I. Balrath.

Balreavie. Baile + riabhach = gray or brindled town.

Balrymonth. Baile + righ + monadh = town of the king's hill. A similar name in the same district is Kilry-month, the old name of St. Andrews.

Balsillie. Baile + saileach = town of willows. I. Currasilla.

Balsusny. *Balsasny.* Baile + Sassonach = the Saxons' town.

Baltilly. *Baltulie.* Baile + tulach = town on the hill.

Balvaird. Baile + bard = bard's town. I. Ballyward.

Balwearie. Baile + maer = town of the *maers* or stewards. Cp. Mairs' land : also Balleweir, with variant Balmoir, in Balquidder. I. Tinwear, I. O. M. Ballavoar.

Balyeoman. I take this to be a rare instance in Scotland of the Irish form of a family name formed by O'. Thus O'Mochain, which would be Anglicised O'Mohan, with baile prefixed, would give Balyeoman ; and it should be noted the name Mochain occurs in Kinross in the name Portmoak.

Banbeath. Baile + beath = town of the birch trees. Ban-at the beginning of names is a contraction of *baile* and *an*, the Celtic article.

Banchory. Beannchor = peaked hill. I. Banagher, Bangor.

Bancliro. Baile + cleireach = priest's town.

Bandene = Ballindene.

Bandirran. *Ballinderran.* Baile + daire = town of the oakwood. I. Ballinderry.

Bandon. Baile + dun = town of the fort.

Bandrum. *Balendrum.* Baile + drum = town on the ridge.

Bangad. Baile + gad = town of the withes.

Bangour. Baile + gobhar = town of the goats.

Bannafield. *Bannockfield.* Banog = little lea field. I. Banoge.

Bannaty. *Bannachtin, Balnechtan.* Baile + Nechtan = Nechtan's town.

Bantuscall. Baile + ant-soisgeul = town of the Gospel. Cp. Pettintoskell.

Barns. Bearnas = a gap in mountains. I. Barnes, Barnismore.

Barnslie. Bearnas + liath = gray hill pass.

Barrington. An English settlement.

Baspard Hill.

Bassaguard. *Bes aiker.*

Beath. Beith = birch tree.

Begg. Beag = little. The noun which was qualified has disappeared, the adjective alone remaining.

Beley. I identify this with old Fife name Ballebelin (A). Beli is the name of a Celtic deity, whence the compound Cunobelinos yielding the Shakespearian Cymbeline. See Belliston.

Belliston. Perhaps a partial translation of Ballebelin (see under Beley). So, according to Bannister's *Cornish Place Names*, Blisland, formerly Bliston, is derived from Beli.

Benarty. *Cabennartye* (A). If this form, given in the Chartulary of St. Andrews, is correct, the explanation may be the same as for Cæsar's Mons Gebenna, Cevennes ; Welsh *cefn*, a ridge. The second part may indicate an Arthurian locality, so that the name would mean Arthur's Ridge, or one of the many Arthur's Seats.

Bennochy. Beannaichte = blessed lands ; beannaichte is a loan-word from Lat. benedictus.

Beverkae. I do not know if this name is old in Fife, but it is evidently from beaver. Cp. English Beverley, Bevercoates, etc.

Bickarton. An English settlement.

Bickramside.

Bighty. A contraction of some name of which the first part is baile, just as Balhouffie came to be called Bowfie, and Balbie, Bawbie.

Binn, The. Beinn = the peak. "Beinn" in Fife generally indicates a pointed summit.

Bishophill. Like Bishopshire, in which it lies, this name originates from the owner being the Archbishop of St. Andrews.

Bishopshire. "Shire" in this name was equivalent to barony. There was a very considerable number of these in Fife, as Lochoreshire, etc. Sheriff Mackay, in his *History of Fife*, suggests the probability of these " shires "originating from ancient Celtic divisions. Bishopshire is thus the barony of the Archbishop of St. Andrews, and comprised the following lands :— Kinnesswood, Powmill, Balgeddie, Kilnagadwood, Kinneston, Balnethil, Portmoak, and Brackly. It is noteworthy that the whole parish of Portmoak, in which Bishopshire lies, was the property of the Church.

Bladdershaw. The shaw or wood of Bladar. See Pitbladdo, Pitbladar.

Blair. Blar = open plain.

Blairathort. *Blairforth*, and so still pronounced. Blair + coirthe = open space of the standing stones. For full explanation see under Milnathort.

Blaircousnie, Blaircurschenye. Blair + corr + shangan = field of the round hill of the anthills. This place is to be identified with the lands afterwards known as Blair ; East Blair being now known, however, as Benarty.

Blairinbathie. *Blairinbothie*. Blar + bothan = field of the huts.

Blairngone. Blar + con = field of the dogs.

Blalowan. Baile + leamhna = town of elms.

Blarnekery. Blar + caorach = open field of the sheep. (A) contains the forms Blaregerog, Blarkeroch, but it is not clear if it is the same place as Blarnekery.

Blawhidder. *Bogwiddy.* Baile + coiteir = town of the cottars. This is approximately the explanation ; the full meaning involves the French word coterie, which Littré points out is derived from cot, and signified a company formed by a number of peasants to hold lands in servile tenure under a lord. Blawhidder (or Balquidder, as it is in Perth) means the town of a coterie or such a peasant club. So also Balquiderock in Stirling.

Blebo. *Blabo, Blabolg, Bladebolg, Blathbolg.* This name is undoubtedly identical in origin with the Blatum Bulgium in the Antonine Itinerary, although the latter is supposed to have been situated in Dumfriesshire. For notes on the latter part of the name see Dunbog.

Blether Burn.

Blindwells. A well supposed to cure blindness.

Blinkbonny. Baile + bainne = milk town.

Blinkeerie. Probably identical with Balekerin (*q.v.*)

Boarhills. *Byrhillis.* Buar = cowshed.

Bogearn. Baile + carn = town of the cairns.

Bogie. *Bolgyne.* These were the lands granted by Macbeth to the Culdees (see A). The word occurs in Dunbog (*Dunbolg*), and in Blebo (Blathbolg). In Gaelic "bolg" means a sack, but the probability is that the name is præ-Celtic, and that the Celts confused it with their own similar word. I. Dunbolg.

Boglile. *Balglelie.* See Balgallyn.

Bonerbo. The last part of this name is identical with Airbow Point. Bun + ard + bogha = end of the height of the bend.

Bonhard. Bun + ard = bottom of the height, or it may be baile + ard = town on the height.

Boreland. *Bordland.* Board + land, *i.e.* mensal land.

Borland.   Same as preceding

Bow of Fife = the bend of Fife.

Bowhouse = Cattlehouse.   Cp. Flockhouse—

> " Bot and he tak' a flok or two,
> A bow of ky."—*Bannatyne Poems.*

Bowpray.   Fr. beau + pré = fine meadow.

Brackly.   *Bracolic.*   Breac + aille = speckled cliffs.

Brandy Burn.   Bran Dubh, an Irish king's name, meaning black raven.

Branxton = town where branks were kept.

Braughty.   Bruach, a bank or border, as in Tignabruaich.

Breadless.   *Burdles, Bredles.*   Broadleys = broad meadows.

Brego, Brago.   Breugach = lying, deceitful ; a common name in Ireland due either to the treachery of bog land or to the swiftness of a mountain torrent in flood.

Broadshade.   Broad shede, *i.e.* a land division.   The word in this sense is from Scandinavian usage.

Brockly.   Brochloch = place of badgers.

Brotus.   Named after St. Protasius or Protus.

Bruckley.   Bruchlag = a wretched hut.

Bruntfield Bray.   This and the following names containing Brunt- indicate where the lands were set on fire for improvement.   The Celtic *loisgte* in names indicates the same practice.

Brunton ; Brunthill ; Bruntshiels.   For each of these see Bruntfield.

Buchadlach.   Baile + Cathlach = Cathlach's town.   Balkaithly is of the same origin.

Buckhaven.   The very strong Teutonic appearance of this name is to be regarded with suspicion.   It appears to attach itself to the old form Backevan, and is a compound of baile and a personal name ; perhaps is town of [M']Ewan.   Note similar corruptions of baile in Bucklyvie, Bogwhiddy, Buchadlach, etc.

Bucklyvie.   *Baldevies, Baldaveyis.*   Baile + claidheamh = town of the sword.

Bullions.   *Bullennes.*   An English pl.   Bullann = a well in a rock.   I. Bullaun.

Bungs (of Cassingray). "Bungs" is an English plural of the next word "Bunzion."

Bunzion. Beinnin, dim. of beann = little peak. I. Binnion, Bignion, Slieve Bingian in the Mourne range.

Burglyn, Burkelin, Borkelin. Barr + Ceallach = Kelly's summit. This is the origin of the name Barclay.

Burleigh. Barr + liath = gray summit.

Burntisland. See Bruntfield.

Burnturk. Bearna + torc = pass of the wild boar. I. Kanturk; -turk shows the inflexion tuirc, genitive of torc.

Burowin. Barr + abhainn = summit of the river. The form Burvane, however, occurs also.

Bussis. A plural form. Probably same name as Bowhouse, i.e. cattlehouse, locally pronounced Boose.

Butter Road. This is a drove road over the Ochils.

Butterwell. The popular explanation is probably the best—a well so cool that it was excellent in buttermaking.

Butts of Scotlandwell. Butt is ground set apart for archery.

Byresloan. See Boarhills.

Caberswallis. The wells of Caber, a personal name which appears in such names as Caberston in Peebles.

Cadham. *Caldhame.* Cold Home.

Caiplie. A form Capa appears in Gaelic signifying a head or point of land, and is cognate with Caput. From this an adjectived form Capleach is derived, whence the above name Caiplie, or as it appears in Ross-shire, Caplich. See Cuplawhills.

Caiplochie. Capa + lochan = head of land by the little loch.

Cairnavain. Cairn + beinn = cairn on the hill.

Cairneubie. Carn + Colban = Colban's cairn.

Cairnsclure. Carn + cluaran = cairn of the thistles. The "s" is a corruption.

Cairnypairt. Carn + barr = cairn of the summit.

Calais. This, like many Fife names, is an English plural of a Celtic name, arising from the fact that lands have been subdivided, *e.g.* into the sunny and the shady halves.   Cala = marshy meadow.

Callange. *Callinche.* I consider this a corruption similar to that in Markinch, Dalginch, and that the original form was Callan, identical with Callain, now Callan, the name of several rivers in Ireland, one of which in Kilkenny gives name to the town of Callan.

Cambo. Ceann + bogha = head of the bend, most descriptive of the situation of Cambo. Cambo, in Roscommon, in Irish Ceann Bugha, shows the same change of " n " to "m " before the labial " b."

Camcase. Cam + casan = winding path.

Cameron. *Camberone.* Cam + bearn = crooked gap or pass.   Cp. Cambusbarron in Stirling.

Camilla. Said to be named after a Countess of Moray.

Campse. Cam = crooked.

Candy. Ceann + dubh = dark head.

Cantsdam. Cant is an old Scottish surname, probably identical with the adjective cant, meaning lively. The great philosopher Kant is said to have been of Scottish descent.

Canzerquhy. (MS).

Capledrae. Capall + traigh = horses' strand. These lands are situated by the Lochty Burn which formed small lochs all now drained.

Cappochs. An English plural. Ceapach = a plot for tillage.   I. Cappog.

Capshard. Capa + ard = high head of land. The " s " is a corruption.

Carberry. Same name as the Irish Carberry, derived from Cairbre, a son of King Niall of the Nine Hostages. It is an instance of the usual Celtic practice of naming lands after a personal name, the reverse process to that of feudal times when personal names were taken from lands.

Cardenden. *Cardonenie.* Cathair + dion = fort of shelter.

Cardsknolls. This name is strong evidence of the English word Knoll being of Celtic origin, a derivative of cnoc (knock). So Cardsknolls would mean the fort on the little hill. The insertion of "ds" is a manifest corruption resulting from an attempt to make the word bear an English meaning.

Carhurly. *Carlchurlie.*

Carmore. Cathair + mor = great fort.

Carnbee. *Carnbeyn.* Carn + binnein = cairn of the peak.

Carnbo. Carn + bo = cairn of the cows.

Carneil. Neil's cairn.

Carngour. Carn + gobhar = goats' cairn.

Carnock. Carnach = abounding in cairns.

Carphin. *Carewyne* (R). Cathair + fionn = the white fort.

Carpow. *Carpully. Kaerfuill.* Cathair + poll = fort of the pool. Cp. Welsh Carphilly.

Carriston. *Carrelston, Karinhalstan,* a name of Scandinavian origin.

Carsegour. *Caskygour.* Casan + gobhar = goat's path. I think " k " is wrong in this name as in Caskieberran.

Carskerdo. Cathair + ciar + dubh = dark gray fort.

Carslogie. *Claslogie.* Clais + lug = trench of the hollow.

Carspersell. Cathair + Breasail = fort of Breasal, for which see under Donibristle, the latter part of which occasionally is written—birsell. The familiar variation illustrated in birsell or brisel is due to the letter " r " being a semi-vowel.

Cartmore. Cathair + mor = great fort.

Carvenom. Cathair + beannan = fort of the little hill.

Carwhingle. Cahir + ceann + geal = fort of the white head. Chingil was the name of a fishing on the Tay.

Carwhinny. Carn + coinnein = cairn of the rabbits. Cp. an old name Carwynninhill in Ayr.

Cash. Cas = foot.

Caskieberran. *Cassabarrean.* Casan + bearn = path of the pass. The letter "k" is inorganic, see Carsegour.

Cassendilly. *Cassindoly.* Casan + duille = leafy, shady path. I. Knockadilly.

Cassindonald. Casan + Domhnall = Donald's path.

Cassingray. Casan + reidh = pass of the plain.

Cast. Cp. Gastdovenald in MS, which however seems to be the present Cassindonald.

Catherie. Cp. the Irish name Tomcatry (Tuaim Cathraigh) now obsolete, but existing in the time of James I.

Catochill. *Kyntochill* (S). This is the Cindocellum of the geographer of Ravenna, and means the head or end of the Ochils.

Caverns. This name is of the same origin as the Border names Cavers, Caverton, Cavens, and Caberton. See Caberswallis.

Cavilston. Gabhail in Gaelic, literally "taking," indicates the ancient Celtic custom of dividing land among a family or a tribe, and the term was probably retained later where the runrig system was observed. So the English local custom (chiefly in Kent) of gavel kind is of Celtic origin, as it stands for gabhail cine = taking by the family, *i.e.* equal division among the sons.

Cecnyflett.

Ceres. *Sireis.* Norse syr + reit = enclosure for swine. For full explanation see Rires.

Chamberfield. The chawmer or chamberlain's field.

Chancefield. See next.

Chance Inn. Change House is an old Sc. term for an ale-house; probably a place where horses were changed.

Channel. See Shanwell, Shambelton, and the Channel of Pittendriech.

Channel, The (of Pittendreich). Sean + baile = old town. See preceding entry.

Chapel. A chapel dedicated to a saint whose name has now disappeared.

Charleton.

Chemises. A modern English plural of old Sc. chemis, O. F. chymois, chef mez, Lat. caput and mansio = chief mansion house. So in (S) there is "Uchtirmerny (Auchtermairnie) *cum le chymmis.* The chemise or principal messuage sould not be devidit" (Balfour's *Practicks*). "The mychty grett Ence, wythin his narrow chymmis leidis he" (Douglas, *Æneis*).

Chesters.

Chewton.   Town of the choughs.

" Chonnane " = " salinagium (Scotice)."   The authority for this name and its explanation is (A) ; " Scotice," of course, means in the Gaelic language.

Clarmonet.   Clar + monadh = plain by the hill.   The " monadh " must have been the name of a specific district near St. Andrews, as there occur also Balry-month and Kilrymonth.   The name is identical with Fr. Clermont.

Claschedeugly.   Clais + dubh + gleann = trench of the dark glen.   Deuglie and Glendeuglie also occur, situated at Glenfarg.

Classlochie.   Clais + lacha = trench or ditch of the ducks.

Clatto.   Cladach = stony beach or river bank.

Claydales.   An English plural.   Cladh + dal = dyke or rampart of the cornland.

Claysike.   Cladh + saighead = rampart of the arrows.

Cleish.   Clais = a hollow or trench, a name very descriptive of the locality.

Clentrie.   *Clyntray.*   Claen + traigh = sloping shore.

Clephanton.   The town of the Clephans.   Clephane is an old Fife family name.   The local pronunciation is Clepan, cp. Clepington near Dundee.

Clocharthaw.   The stone of Arthur (cloch = stone), an Arthurian locality.   See Pittarthie and Craigarter.

Clochrat (bridge).   Clach + rath = stone of the fort.   The place is close to the ruins of Inchgall Castle.

Clockmydron.   In the Black Book of Carmarthen there occurs the name Mabon son of Mydron.   Mabon is supposed to give name to Lochmaben, and there is a stone there known as Clochmaben ; in the same way Clochmydron may be the stone of Mydron.   It should be noted, however, that the place name Dron occurs in the same district.

Clubstone.   Cp. Clubscross near Peterhead.   It may indicate spots where social meetings took place.

Clune.   Cluain = meadow.

Clunievar.   Cluain + fear = meadow of the men.

Clunvan. Cluain + ban = white meadow.

Cluny. Cluain = meadow.

Clushford. Clais + fuar = cold trench.

Clushgreen. Clais + grian = sunny hollow.

Cnocenlein. Cnoc + lin = flax hill.

Coalpitden. Coille + poite + dion = wood of the hollow of the place of shelter. Cp. Coilpotburne near Falkland where there are no coalpits.

Coates. In all the Brythonic dialects the ordinary word for a wood is a form which appears in Welsh *coit* (Mod. W. coed), Corn. *cuit*, Bret. *coat*. The existence of this word in Irish is shown by a word in an early MS, ciadeholum, the gloss being *palumbes, i.e.* wood-pigeons. The name Coates contains the same word, I think, especially when the names Coitt, Coitmure, Balcuty mire, and Kinneswood are considered. The word occurs in the rare Latin word bu-cetum, a pasture for cattle; the etymological equivalent in English is heath.

Cockairnie. Culcarny. Cul + probably Gairney, a stream flowing into Lochleven. If so, the meaning is the back of Gairney. There is another Cockairnie near Aberdour. Coolcarney in Ireland, Cuil Cearnadha as written in Irish, is derived from a personal name.

Cockamy. Cuil + caime = corner of the winding place.

Cogfauld.

Coilpot (burne), near Falkland. Coille + poite = wood of the hollow.

Coitmure = great wood. See Coates.

Coldon. Cul + dun = back of the fort.

Coldrain. *Collandraine, Condraine.* Cul + draighean = back of the thorns.

Collairnie. *Callernie.* Cul + airne = back of the sloes. I. Killarney.

Collessie. Cul + lios = back of the garden ground. The neighbouring name of Pitlessie indicates that the second component is -lessie, not -essie.

Colliston. Collinstoun = Collins' toun.

Colluthie. *Calluthie.*

C

Collydean.

Collyford.

Colzie. Coilltean, plural of coille = wood. See Balhoussie.

Comerton. Cummers' town.

Comrie. Comar = confluence.

Conaty. Identical with Irish Connaught. Casconity is also an old Fife name.

Conland. *Condillan, Condolane.* This is the Irish name Dillon with the common Celtic prefix in personal names Con. Cp. the Welsh Cynddylan, and see Contle.

Contle. *Quintall.* This is identical with the personal name familiar in Irish literature, Condla or Condle, which is the same as Condollios, a name found in a Roman inscription at Saalburg. Cp. also Conland.

Cormodle (a hill in the Ochil range). *Cormoddil, Carmodle.* There is a Carmodil in the Isle of Man. The latter part is probably a personal name, and may be Motla, king of the Deises of Munster, mentioned in the Annals of Ulster (K).

Cornceres. This name does not appear early. It seems to consist of the English word corn and ceres, indicating a place where corn was specially grown or stored, just as Corntown occurs in Scotland. See Ceres.

Corrinzion. Corr + iongan = round top of the peaked hill. See Ingan.

Corston, *i.e.* Crosstoun.

Cothegellie. Coit + gile = wood of brightness. See Coates.

Cotton, The (*e.g.* of Dura). Coitchionn = commonty. I. Cutteen, Ardcotten, Ballycotton.

Coul. Cuil = corner.

Coultra. *Cultrach.* Cul + traigh = back of the shore.

Countryhills. Probably a corruption of the same word as appears in Contlaw in Aberdeen.

Couston.

Cowbakie. The first part of this name is cul = back.

Reading the latter part of the name along with the name Kembak I take it to be the same as the Irish place name Bac in Mayo; it was divided into two parts which, a native in 1838 informed O'Donovan, were called Cul-Bhac and Beal-Bhac. The former of these is then the same as Cowbakie. Bac means a bend, and Cowbackie is the back of the bend.

Craigancroon. Carraig + crun = rock of the hollow.

Craigarter. Carraig + Arthur, the rock of Arthur, an Arthurian locality.

Craigduckie. Carraig + scabhac = hawks' craig.   I. Craigatuke.

Craigencalt. Carraig + gealt = rock of the lunatics.   I. Tobernagalt.

Craigencat. Carraig + cat = rock of the wild cats.

Craigencrow. Carraig + cro = rock of the sheep-fold.

Craigen Gaw. Carraig + catha = rock of the chaff. Winnowing would be done on the top of a hill.   I. Cavanacaw.

Craiggaveral.

Craiginwar. Carraig + fear = rock of the men.   I. Carrignavar.

Craiglour. Carraig + lobhar = rock of the lepers.

Craigmiglo. Carraig + meigeallaich = rock of the bleating of goats. Near the site of Craigmiglo occurs the name Knaggour, i.e. goats' hill.   See Strathmiglo.

Craignegreen. Carraig + grian = sunny rock.

Craigow. Carraig + co = rock of the yew tree.

Craigrothie. The latter part of the name, Rothie, is the same word as appears in Rothes, Rothiemurchus, Rothiemay; it probably represents ruadhag, a young roe.

Craigsanquhar. Carraig + scan + cathair = rock of the old fort.

Craigsimmie.

Crail. *Karel, Karale.* Probably identical with the Irish name Cairill and the family name O'Carroll.   See Elie.

Crainbrigis.

Crambeth. Crom + beth = crooked birch tree.

Crannoch. Crannach = abounding in trees, or it may mean a wooden house. I. Crannog.

Crawness. For Crawnest, Crow Nest.

Creich. Crioch = boundary, or district.

Crockmuirhall. The first part of this name is cnoc (knock) = hill, and it represents the modern Gaelic pronunciation, "cn" being pronounced "cr."

Croftgary.

Crosshill. Probably so called from a cross being placed on it ; the chapel of Inchgall was near.

Crownarland. Land of the crownar or coroner, an office now not known in Scotland. For the form cp. Shakespeare "crowner's inquest."

Cruivie. Craobh = tree.

Cuffabout. Cp. Tailabout.

Culbyne. From the personal name Colban. See Rescobie, Cairncubie.

Cullalo. *Cullelouch, Culzelauche.* "Z" in the last form stands for "g," so that the name is cul + dha + loch = back of the two lochs. Dha is the separated form of da and is pronounced approximately ga.

Culross. *Culenross, Culrois.* This may represent the name of a King Culan who was killed in the Lothians and buried "by the brink of the waves." The meaning would be thus Culan's promontory.

Cultbuy (now Bouton, in Kinross). Coillte + buidhe = yellow woods.

Cults. English plural of *coillte*, itself the plural of coille = wood.

Cummerknowe. Comer originally meant a godmother, then an associate or gossip ("gossip" itself having the same history), and then a female generally, as "What's a' the steer, kimmer?"

Cummerland. See Cummerknowe.

Cummer Law. See Cummerknowe.

Cunnoquhie. *Cunoquhay.* Perhaps identical with the obsolete forms *Canzerquhy, Cansequhy, Kingsoquhyc.*

Cunyngairland (*vulgo* "Brint-Eland"). Coinicer = rabbit warren. I. Cunnigare. See Nickery.

Cupar.   Cul + barr = back of the top.

Cuplahills.   Capa + law = the point of the law.   The word law is Celtic as well as Teutonic.   Cp. Couplaw in Lanark, Capelaw in the Pentlands, and Coplawhill in Glasgow.

Cuthilmuir.   Cuttle or cuthil is a Scottish word meaning to carry corn from a low damp situation to higher and drier ground, and secondarily the spot to which it was carried.

Cuttlehill.   See preceding.

Cutty Hillock.   Cuttie is a Scottish term for a hare.

Dalachy.   *Dalcho, Delcho, Dachie* (the last form representing the present local pronunciation).   Dealgach = thorny.

Dalgairn.   Dal + carn = field of cairns.

Dales.   See Dolyland.

Dalgetie.   Dalgathie.   Dal + gath = field of spears.

Dalginch.   *Dalgins.*   This name exhibits the same corruption as appears in Markinch and in the spelling Callinch for Callenge.   It is derived from the personal name Delga, from which Dundalk is named, this being Dun-Dealgan, *i.e.* the fort of Delga, a Firbolg chief.

Dalquhamie.   Dal + caime = field by the windings.   Cp. Cockamie

Dargus.   Dearg = red.

Darnwe.   This seems to be the same place as is indicated by the obsolete names Derno, Darnoch, Dornoche.   Doirneag = pebbly.

Dattie Mill.   Inschdattie Milne.   From the plural of dabhoch, a land measure.   See Findatie.

Demons.   *Demungis.*   This is a corruption of demesne, the lands occupied by the lord of the manor himself.   Cp. Dymyns and Le Demmyns in Cornwall.

Demperston.   The town of the dempster.

Dennimonkshill.

Denork.   *Dunorc.*   This name associates itself with the Fife names Orkie and Orrock, and the obsolete Orkvenay (R).   The latter part of the name is most probably a Scandinavian name which also gave name to the Orkney islands, so that the usual etymology of Orkney from Celtic orc (porcus), meaning a whale (lit. pig), would be erroneous.

Deuglie. *Duglyn.* Dubh + gleann = dark glen.

Devilla. Dubh + illann = black island.

Devilly Burn. See Devilla.

Devon. Dubh + abhainn = dark river. One of the two rivers of this name is still called the Black Devon. It should be noted that while this district was anciently inhabited by a tribe named Dumnonii, Devonshire in England was occupied by a tribe of a similar name, Damnonii. The old spelling of Devon in the name of the village Crook of Devon is Dovan.

Dillycary.

Dochrie Hill.

Dollais. See Dolyland.

Dolls Park. See Dolyland.

Dolyland or **Doleland**, The, of Cleish. This name is now obsolete, but the same word appears in the Fife names, Dales, Doll's Park, and Dollais. Dale or Dole indicated portions of fields marked off by landmarks, no doubt for arable purposes. There is a Doll's Park on the estate of Kirkness, and the local tradition is that it was land set apart for the poor (*doled out* to them).

Donibristle. *Donybirsell.* Dun + Breasal = the fort of Breasal, an Irish personal name, whence the family name O'Breasal and the title in the Irish peerage, Clanbrassil. Bresel or brisil is one of the Breton words in the Charters of the Abbey of Beauport, and is explained as meaning war. Cp. Carspersell.

Dothan. *Dovan.* Dubhachan = black land. I. Dooghan.

Douranside. Douran is for Dobharan a diminutive of dobhar, water. The word appears more fully in the Scottish river name Doveran ("bh" is the Gaelic equivalent of "v"), and it appears in a more contracted form in Bundoran in Ireland, and in Craigendoran in Dumbarton. Douran represents the original form better than Doran.

Dovolay. The latter part of this obsolete name contains the same element as the Fife names Travalay, Banaley, also obsolete. Banaley occurs in Midlothian in the form of Bonally. Cp. the name Dovellie in Inverness.

Drinkbetween. This may be a corruption of an old Fife name (MS) Duncbrenan, *e.g.* Brenan's fort.

Dron. *Dran.* Dronn (a derivative form from drum) = back.

Drumcarro. *Drumcarachin.* Drum + carrach = rough ridge.

Drumchaldy. Drum + coillte = ridge of the woods.

Drumcooper. Drum + cul + barr. See Cupar.

Drumdreill. *Drumdaill, Drumdoill, Drumdile.* " R " in the second part of the word is wrongly inserted from sympathy with the " r " in drum. Drum + dall = blind-man's ridge.

Drumeldrie. *Drummeleric.* Drum + iolaire = eagles' ridge.

Drumfin. Drum + fin = white ridge.

Drumgarland. *Drumgarlet.* Drum + gearr + leathad = short ridge of the hill side.

Drumlochethornoche, Drumlochdurnoch, Drumlochirnoch. This name is now obsolete, but it appears to be the origin of the name Lochran, in the same locality. Drum + loch + doirneag = ridge of the pebbly loch.

Drumly. Drum + liath = gray ridge.

Drummain. Dromainn – little ridge. I. Drummans. In later times the name is Englished Drummond.

Drummaird. Drum + airde = ridge of the height.

Drummochy. *Drumoquhy.* Drum + achadh = ridge of the field.

Drumnagoil. Drum + gall = ridge of the strangers—-nagoil is the genitive of *gall* preceded by the def. article. It is one of the many illustrations of the accurate reproduction in the earlier English spellings of the modification of vowels indicating the Celtic inflexions. The formation of the goil from gall is illustrated in English by such plural forms as mice from mouse.

Drumnod. Drum + foid = ridge of the grassy surface.
Drumraik. *Drumrawak.* Cp. Kilraike.
Drumranet. Drum + roinn = ridge of the divisions or portions.
Drumrichnak. Drumrechmak.
Drumshandry. This is the name of a field on an old plan of Kirkness. Drum + scan + drui = ridge of the old Druid. I. Loughnashandree.
Drumtenant.
Drumtrissil.
Drumtuthil. Drum + Tuathal = the ridge of Tuathal. Tuathal is the origin of the name O'Toole or Toole.
Drunzie. Drungan = meeting of a tribe. I. Drung ; "z" for "g" frequently occurs, and is due to a misreading of old styles, e.g. Inzievar, formerly Ingefair. "Drungan" is cognate with English "throng."
Duchrone. Dochteroun. Dabhach + tioram = dry davock.
Duloch. Dubh + loch = black loch.
Dullomuir. Dubh + loch = black loch.
Dumbarnie. Dun + bearna = fort of the pass.
Dumbarro. *Dunberauch.* The latter part of this name is an adjective form from barr, summit, so that the name means fort on the summit.
Dumghercloihe. Dun + gearr + clach = fort of the short rock.
Dummiefarline. This is on a summit of the Cleish hills, 1022 ft. high, where there are the remains of a fort. The name is evidently the fort of [Mac] Farlane. See Dunfermline.
Dunbog. *Dunbolg.* See Bogie. I. Dunbolg.
Duncrievie. Dun + craobh = fort of the trees.
Dunduff. Dun + dubh = black fort.
Dunearn. Dunarne. The latter part of this name is identical with the Scottish river named Earn and the Irish Erne, all pointing back to the name of Ireland, so that Duncarn is really the fort of Erin.
Dunfermline. The fort of [Mac] Farlane. See Dummiefarline.
Dunglow. Dun + gleo = fort of strife. I. Dunglow.

Dunimarle. Dun + meirlech = robbers' fort.

Dunino. *Duneynauche.* Dun + aonach = fort on the uncultivated heath.

Dunnahaglis. Dun + eaglais = fort of the church.

Dunniefard. Dun + fear = fort of the men.

Dunniface. Dun + paiste = fort of the charmed serpents. Cp. Kilface.

Dunnikeir. *Denekery.* Dun + Ciarraidhe = fort of the tribe of Ciar (whence Kerry in Ireland).

Dunnygask. *Tunygask,* and probably *Teykingask.* Tech + ceann + gasg = house of the head of the tail.

Dunotter. Kincardineshire Dunottar stands for Dunfothir, but the Fife one should be connected with the Scandinavian Ottir, as in Otterston and in Pittottar.

Dunshalt.

Dura. Like a Dowray in Ayr this name is a contraction of Dollywraa = the enclosure of the Doleland. See Dolyland and Rires.

Durdam.

Durie.

Dysart. Lat. Desertum, a place of retirement for religious purposes. It is a common name in Ireland frequently joined with the name of a saint.

Earnieside. Of the same origin as the River Earn, Duncarn, Lough Erne, and Erin *i.e.* Ireland.

Eden. *Edyne.* Aodann = brow ; so called, probably, because the river rises at the brow of the W. Lomond Hill.

Edindowny. Idindawny. Aodann + dunan = brow of the little fort. Cp. Edyndonyng in Perth. The spelling Idindawny indicates the conflict between "e" and "i" to represent Gaelic "ao."

Eglismaly. Eglismaldie, another name for Buchadlach, and it means Church of St. Malie. Cp. Kilmalie in Argyll and the old name of the parish of Golspie, Culmallie. There was also an Eglismaldy in Kincardine.

Eglismartene.   St. Martin's Church, old name for Strathmiglo.

Elie (formerly known as The Elie, and still locally so). Several tribes in Ireland took name from an ancestor Eile, and the districts occupied by them came to be known by the same name, each being distinguished by the addition of a family or clan name. Thus Ely O'Carroll is the Ely of the O'Carrolls.   See Crail.

Endoreth.   (A).

Eschewyn.   Cp. Ashes and Foodieash.

Esky Loch.   Iasg = fish ; loch well stocked with fish.

Falfield and **Falside.**   See Faluhill.   These names show that in Old English the forms fal and falu occurred just as in Modern German fahl and falb.

Falkland.   Land of falconry ; the ancient name of the parish is Kilgour.

Faluhill.   The first part of this term is a Teutonic word meaning pale yellow.   It appears in modern German as fahl and falb.   In Old English it was fealu and fealo.   The modern English fallow is a derived sense from the colour of unploughed land, or " red land " as it is locally termed.   The word is identical in origin with Lat. palidus, Gr. πολιός, Sansk. palita.

Falulecche.   For the first part see Faluhill ; the last part is an old form of lea.

Fargie.   *Fourgie.*   Fuar + ceann = cold head.

Feal, The.   Faill = cliff.

Feddinch = Feddins, an Eng. pl. of feadan = little stream.   I. Feddan.

Fernie, Farnie.   Fearn = alder.   I. Farnagh, Fernie.

Ferry-Port-on-Craig.   In (B) Petencraig.   Port is probably a corruption of Pit, as in the case of Portmoak, *q.v.*, so the name would mean portion of the rock.

Fervenshyre or **Foirvinschip** is described as being a " prebenda " of Abernethy.   Fuar + beann = cold hill.

Fetters.   This is an English plural form of a Celtic term for a stream.   I. Fethernagh.

Fettykill.   *Fythkill.*   Fitheach + coille = raven's wood.

Feus (*e.g.* of Drunzie). English plural of fiodh = wood.
I. The Fews, a barony in Armagh.

Fife. The name represents Fib, one of the eponymous
sons of Cruithne.

Findatie. *Findauchty.* Fionn + dabhach = fair davochs (a
measure). The name occurs also in Elgin Findochty
and in Sutherland Davockfin, the adjective in the
latter case being last.

Finderly. Fionn + larach = fair-coloured site. Cp. Ma-
cherrderly for Macharlary.

Fingask. Fionn + gasg = fair-coloured tail. Earball,
another term for "tail" is also often used in place
names.

Finglassie. Fin + glaise = fair stream. I. Finglas.

Flass. Cp. Flashadder, *i.e.* Flass Water in Berwick.

Flisk. Fleasc occurs in O'Davoren's Irish glossary with
the meaning "traigh," *i.e.* shore. This meaning corre-
sponds with the situation of Flisk. There is a river
in Kerry named Flesk.

Fluris. A plural form ; Fr. fleur = flower.

Fluthers. *Flotteris.* Fluthers is a Fife term for flakes
from laminated rocks (Jamieson).

Fod. Foid = a peat.

Foodie. *Futhie.* Fodagh = a soddy or grassy place.

Foodieash. Cp. preceding, and for termination cp.
Ashes.

Fordel. Fordall = fore or front dale.

Forgan.

Formonthills. *Foirmanhillis.* Fuar + monadh = cold
hill.

Forret. *Forrat.* Same as personal name Ferat (K).

Forthar. Of the same origin as the name of the river
Forth and of the village Forth in Lanarkshire, also
Forth in Ireland. The name is derived from the
legendary person Fothart. In Forth the "r" is
misplaced.

Fossoway. Fasach + mach = desert of the plain.

Fotheris. Fothar = forest.

Fothryff or **Fothreve.** Fothar = forest. A similar ter-

mination occurs in Moravia, Moray. Fothryff was a
district including West Fife and Kinross, and it is
known historically from (R) that there was a forest of
Kinross.

Foulford. Dirty ford.

Foulhogger.

Foulthumbs.

Fourlums. An Eng. pl. Fuar + lann = cold land.

Foxton. No doubt identical with the old name Folkes-
toun. So in I. O. M. Folkesdale has become Fox-
dale. Cp. Folkstone in England.

Freelands. These lands are situated in the parish of
Ceres, and may be identical with "the Frieland of
Lindors." The name indicates land free from rent or
services. So in Ireland the name Serse is derived
from saeirse, a noun derived from saer, free. See
Sireisland.

Freuchie. Fraoch = heather.

Friarton. Town of friars.

Fruix. *Fruchtis.* An English plural of fraoch = heather.
The explanation of these English plurals is that
lands were generally divided into parts, *e.g.* the sunny
and the shady halves, hence a plural was formed to
describe all the parts collectively.

Gadvan. Cp. the name Cadvan, king of N. Wales. The
first part of the name is cath = war, and the name
evidently means warrior.

Gallatown. Probably the same as the Fife name given
in (S), Galloustoun, *i.e.* town of the Gallows.

Garpit. Gearr + poite = short hollow.

Gartary. Gart + airidh = garden of the herd. Gart or Gort
in Irish, meaning enclosure, is etymologically the same
as Lat. hortus and Eng. garden. In modern Scots it
assumes the form of "yard," as in kailyard, meaning a
cottager's garden (a different word from the lineal
measure). In Slavonic it assumes the form of gorod,
as in Novgorod = New Town.

Gartwhinzean. Gart + Congan = Congan's garden or enclosure.

Garvock. Garbh = rough. I. Garvagh = rough land.

Gask. Gasg = tail. Cp. the use of earball with same meaning in place names. There must have been also an adjectival derivative, as Gaskie Hill occurs near Dunfermline, and Gasgow Park is the name of a field on Kirkness estate.

Gaskinienemphy. Gasg + ionga + fionn = tail of the white-pointed rock. See Ingan.

Gathercauld. Cathair + coille = fort of the wood.

Gauldry. *Gallery, Galuran.* For the termination cp. the name Kelturan in (K).

Gellet. *Gullet.* This word, literally meaning throat, (Lat. gula), indicates a narrow channel worn by water, and sometimes the small stream itself. The word is now better known in the form gully. See Gullet Bridge.

Gelvan. Geal + beann = white hill.

Glac. Glac = hollow. I. Glack.

Gladney. Glaidnie. I. Gladney, Co. Down.

Glanderstoun. Gillander's town.

Glencortas.

Glencraig. *Cluncraig.* Claon + carraig = meadow of the rock.

Glenduckie. It is difficult to say if this is not the same place as Glenduogin (MS). The latter name seems to have been in the same district. The name may be gleann + dubh + ceann = glen of the dark head.

Glenduogin. (MS).

Glendy. Gleann + dubh = dark glen.

Glenfarg = Glen of the Farg river. This must be associated with the place name in the same district Fargie, Fourgie, *q.v.* Celtic river names often take name from the spot where they rise.

Glenshee. Gleann + sidh = fairy glen.

Glenshervie Moor. Glen is here probably a corruption of cluain (cp. Glencraig). Cluain + searbh = dandelion meadow.

Glentarkie. Gleann + torc = wild boar's glen.

Glenvale. Cluain + faill = meadow below the cliffs. See Feal.

Goatmilk. *Gatmilk.* The first part suggests the name Cait or Got, one of the eponymous sons of Cruithne or the Pict (Caithness, etc.), and the latter part Meilochon, a form of Maglocunos, I. Maelcon, W. Maelgwn. Goatmilk was one of the old "shires."

Golland. This name is derived from a diminutive form of gabhal = fork. It indicates the land in the fork formed by two rivers. I. Golan, Gowlan.

Golloch Hill. Coileach = grouse hill.

Golstoun. The same name as Gaulstoun in Ireland, a partial translation of Ballingall, *q.v.*

Gospetry. *Kilkespardyn. Kilcospardy.*

Gott. A dirty meadow ; hence the adjective "guittery" = miry.

Goudierannet. Cul + da + roinnte = back of the two divisions.

Gowkhall. Cuach = cuckoo.

Growokys Wel (A). This was the name of the spring whence the river Lochty rises on Benarty Hill. This is evidently the Well of Gruoch, Macbeth's queen. It is recorded that Macbeth and Gruoch granted the neighbouring lands of Kirkness to the Culdees.

Guardbridge.

Gullet Bridge. This is the name of a bridge over the new cut made for the river Leven (1827-32) for the first few miles of its course. The name is derived from the mode of capturing the eels in the old river Leven. These fishings belonged to Bishopshire, and in (S) the subjects are described as "*lie* Cruvis alias *lie* Gulatis." Literally the word means throat, and is taken from the French "goulet," which signifies a contrivance by which fish after entering a place cannot escape.

Gutterhole. Guittery hole = miry hole.

Haknakel. Achadh + coille = field of the wood.

Halcatis. "Hall" prefixed to names indicates the hall or manorhouse.

Harelaw.

Harestanes. In England the word appears as hoarstones; they are said to be landmarks.

Hatchbank.

Hattonburn. Aiteann = furze.

Higham. Heichame = high home. Cp. Letham.

Hilcarny.

Hillary, *Haliry, Haligric, Halyrig* = holy ridge, *i.e.* ridge belonging to the Church.

Hisseldean. Hissel for hirsell, hyrsale, hirdsel, is an old Scottish word meaning a multitude or flock. It is cognate with herd and German heerde.

> "The herds and hissels were alarmed."—*Burns.*

Hoill. This name indicates land lying in a hollow.

Humbie = town of the Homes.

Hungrie Hills. Cp. Hungrie Hill in Kerry; it may contain the name of the Pictish King Hungus, just as Countryhillis may contain the name Contan. Hungriflet was also a Fife name.

Hurlmachan.

Hurly.

Inch. This represents the Gaelic inis, often meaning island, and perhaps cognate with Lat. insula. But the word is also very generally applied to a river meadow or good pasture ground.

Incharvie. Inis + tarbh = bulls' meadow.

Inchcolm. Inch of Columba.

Inchcurbrig. Inis + cor + breac = inch of the speckled hill.

Inchdairnie. Inis + dair = inch of the oaks.

Inchegay. Inis + gedh = goose inch.

Inchkerie. Inis + caorach = sheep meadow. I. Inishkeeragh.

Inchminnolein ("cum capella Buchadlach nunc Eglismaldie nuncupata ").

Inglistarvet.   Tarvet belonging to Inglis, subsequently called Scotstarvet.

Ingrie.

Inneans, The.   Summits on the Cleish hills.   Inneoin = anvil.   I. Mullaghnoney = hill top of the anvils.

Innerbridge.

Innergellie.   Mouth of the Gelly.

Inschelt.   Inis + eilit = hind's island.

Inverdovat.   Dubh + ath = dark ford.   The name Cassindoveth also occurs, meaning the path by the dark ford.

Inverie.   *Invary, Inweary*, the form *Finvirie* also occurs. St. Monan is said to have been buried here.

Inverkeithing.   See Dalkeith.

Inverlochtie.   Inbhir + Lochtie = at the mouth of the Lochtie.   This is the earlier name of the lands of Spittell ; " Inverlochtie *alias* Spittell."

Inverteil.   *Invirtule* = mouth of the river Tiel, from tuil = torrent.   See Auchtertool.

Inzievar.   Ingefair.   Ionga + fear = the nail (*i.e.* the pointed rock) of the men.   I. Duninga.

Iratlengre, Schyra de.   This appears to have been in the district of Markinch.   The first part is oireacht = inheritance.   Cp. I. Iraghticonnor = Connor's inheritance.

Jamphlars.

Jargomyre.   Dearg = red.

Justinglands.   Lands where jousting was practised.

Kaikinch, Calkinsh.   Probably derived from a personal name Calcan in the same way as Markinch from Marcan.   The name occurs also in Aberdeen.

Kaim.   Caime = a winding or bend.

Keavil.   See Cavil.

Kectethin.

Kedlock.   *Keithlok, Caithloch*.   This name forms the latter part of such names as Balkaithly, Pitkeathly, Buchadlach.   It is identical with the personal name Cathlach, derived from cath, signifying battle. The name appears in Dumfries as Caitloch.

Kellie. This name is identical with the Irish personal name Ceallach, Englished Kelly.

Kemback. *Kinbak, Kinbuc.* Ceann + bac = head of the bend. See Cowbakie.

Kenleygreen. Ceann + liath = gray head.

Kenniker.

Kennoway. Ceann + mach = head of the plain. I. Cannaway.

Kethyn. See Dalkeith.

Kettle. Cital is a diminutive of the Irish personal name Cet, which appears in Scotland in such names as Keith and Caithness. I. Carrigkittle, Dunkettle.

Kilbrackmont. Coille + breac + monadh = speckled wood of the hill.

Kilconquhar. Coille + Cunuchar = wood of Cunuchar or Cunchar. This was the name of a thane of Angus. The name is pronounced Kinneuchar. Cunuchar is possibly the same as Conchobhar or Connor. See Balgonar.

Kildonyng. Coille + dunan = wood of the little fort.

Kilduff. Coille + dubh = dark wood. See Dowhill.

Kilduncan. Coille + Donncha = Duncan's Wood.

Kilface. Coille + paiste = wood of the charmed serpents. See Dunniface.

Kilgowne. Coille + gamhain = wood of the stirks or yearling cattle. See Balgownie.

Killernie. Coille + airne = wood of the sloes. I. Killarney.

Killiecrankie.

Killraike. This name is identical with Kilravock in Ross, which is pronounced as Kilraike. Cp. Drumraik.

Kilmagadwood. *Kilgad.* Coille + gad = wood of the withes.

Kilmany. Coille + Maine = wood of Maine. Maine was the ancestor of the Irish tribe of Hy Many, which literally means grandsons, *i.e.* descendants of Maine, but is transferred to indicate the territory inhabited by the tribe.

Kilmaron. Coille + mor + beinn = wood of the great hill.

Kilminning. *Kilmonane, Kilmounane.* Church of St. Monan.

Kilmumkyn ("de Karel"). A name Balmoumkin also existed in Fife.

Kilmundie. Coille + muine = wood of the shrubbery.

Kilmux. *Kilmoukis.* This name is an English plural. Coille + muc = wood of pigs.

Kilnynane. *Kilninian.* Coille + eun = wood of birds.

Kilquhiss. *Kilquhous, Kilquhase, Kilquische.* Coille + cos = wood at the foot.

Kilrenny. *Kilretheni.* Coille + raithne = ferny wood. 1. Kilrainy, Lisrenny. The now personal names Rainy, Ranaghan, are taken from the latter part of this word.

Kilrie. Coille + reidh = wood of the plain.

Kinaldy. Ceann + allt = head of the burn.

Kincairny. Ceann + carn = head abounding in cairns.

Kincaple. Ceann + capall = head of the horses.

Kinchaldy. Ceann + coillte = head of the woods.

Kincraig. Ceann + carraig = head of the rock.

Kindargog. Ceann + edar + gag = head between the cleft.

Kingask. Ceann + gasg = head of the tail.

Kinghorn. Ceann + cearn = head of the corner.

Kinglassie. Ceann + glaise = head of the stream.

Kinkell. Ceann + coille = head of the wood.

Kinloch. *Kindelouche.* Ceann + da + loch = head of the two lochs.

Kinloss.

Kinnaird. Ceann + ard = head of the height.

Kinnear. Ceann + iar = western head.

Kinnedar. Ceann + edar, literally "head between," the word to complete the description being omitted.

Kinnesswood. *Keaneskwood.* The local pronunciation is still "Kinascut." The name seems to be ceann + cas + ciad = head of the waterfall of the wood. See Coates.

Kinneston.

Kinninmonth. Ceann + monadh = head of the hill.

Kinsleith. *Kinsleif.* Ceann + sleibh = head of the hill. "Slieve," which occurs so frequently in the topography of Ireland is rare in Scotland, Ben superseding it.

Kippo. *Kippoke* = a place full of stumps of trees. I. Kippagh. Lat. cippus.

Kirkcaldy. *Kircalethin, Kircaladinit.* Cathair + Calaten = the fort of Calaten. The sons of Calaten were famous magicians mentioned in the Book of Leinster. See *Revue Celtique III.*, p. 175. Calaten's sons are also spoken of in the Book of the Dean of Lismore.

Kirkforthar. See Forthar. K. was formerly a parish, but is now merged in Markinch.

Kirklands. Churchlands.

Kirkmay. For the latter part of the word cp. the Isle of May.

Kirkness. These lands, lying in the south-eastern end of Portmoak parish, are mentioned in the first entry in the Chartulary of St. Andrews, and were for a long period Church property. The name is of Teutonic origin, meaning the ness or promontory of the church. The locality, however, in no way accords with this meaning. But in the Constabulary of Crail there was the Kirkness, and there appears to have been a Kirkness near Balmerino. The Church seems, therefore, to have transferred to these lands the name of an earlier possession on the coast, and so superseded an old Celtic name. In contrast to this, here, as in many places, the fields bear old Celtic names, *e.g.* Drumshandry, *q.v.*

Kirkshotts. A place where archery was practised near the church.

Kitchengreen. Coitchionn + grian = sunny commonty.

Kittadie.

Knabs. Cnap = round hillock. I. Knappagh.

Knaggour. Cnoc + gobhar = goats' hill. I. Knocknagower.

Knightsward. Ward is a small piece of enclosed pasture for young animals. So Priorsward in Kirkness.

Knockas.   Cnoc + cas = hill of the waterfall.

Knockcannon.   Cnoc + ceann + fhionn = hill of the white head.   I. Foilcannon, Carrigcannon.

Knockintinny.   Cnoc + teine = hill of the fire.

Knocknary.   Cnoc + aedhaire = shepherd's hill.   I. Corra-narry.

Knocksodrum.   *Knoksuderon.*   Cnoc + sudaire = tanner's hill.   I. Ballynasuddery, Knockatudor.

Knoklargauch, *i.e.* Largo Law.   See Largo.

Knokmadyr.   Cnoc + meadar = hill of the mead cup. Cp. I. Drumnamether, Rathmadder ; also Mathernock in Renfrew.

Kyngarroch.   Ceann + carrach = rough head.

Lacesston, Laucesston.   This may be the same name as Launceston in Cornwall, a corruption of Lann + Stephen = St. Stephen's Church.

Ladeddie.   Leathad + aodann = breadth of the hill brow.

Ladisfrone.   (T).

Lahill.   *Lachillis.*   Leamh + coille = elm wood.   I. Laughil.   See Lucheld.

Lambflatt = lambs' meadow.

Lamboletham.   *Lambeisletham.*   Letham, *q.v.*, belonging to Lamb.

Lappie.   Leaba = bed, grave, monument.   I. Labby.

Larennie.   Leathad + raithneach = ferny breadth.

Largo.   *Largauch.*   Leargach = sunny, seaward slope. Knoklargauch also occurs, an old name for Largo Law.   I. Largy.

Lassindock.

Lassodie.   This name suggests the names Lessuden, an old name of St. Boswells, and perhaps Lasswade. Lios + aodann = garden on the hill brow.

Lathallan.   Leathad + aluinn = beautiful slope.   The form Lathalmond also occurs.   If the latter form is the true one, the last part is amhuinn = river, as in the Almond river in Linlithgow, the word being cognate with Lat. amnis.   In a later form it appears as Avon.

Lathockar. Leathad + ucaire = slope of the fuller. Cp. Pitteuchar. I. Knockanooker.

Lathones. An English plural. Leathad + abhainn = slope by the river.

Lathrisk. *Lothreskey.* Leathad + riasc = breadth of the marsh.

Lathro. This name is the same as the Irish Lathrach, now Laragh, meaning a site, and so indicating the ruins of an ancient building.

Lathrogall. Lathrach + gall = site of the stranger. See Lathro.

Lauer. Leamh = elm. Cp. Laueran, an old name in Dumbarton.

Leckerstone. This name is usually derived from the Teutonic leich = dead body, indicating a spot where funerals rested. But the probability is greater that it is derived from the Celtic leac = a slab or flagstone, and that "stone" affixed to the name is merely a repetition of the meaning in English, See Lykyrstyne and Liquorstone.

Ledenurquhart. Leathad + urchair = breadth of the cast or throw, a name indicating an expanse where the athlete exhibited his skill in throwing.

Ledlanet. An old name occurs, Ledlewnule, which appears to be the same place. If so, -lanet represents leamhan = elm tree. See Lochleven.

Ledlation. *Ladglaschun.* Leathad + glaisin = breadth of the little stream. I. Ardglushin.

Leirhope. "Hope" is a Norse term for an anchorage. "Leir" associates itself with Lerwick.

Leslie. *Leslyn.* Lios + linn = garden of the pool.

Letham. Laigh + ham = the low-lying dwelling. Cp. Higham.

Lethangie. Leathad + teanga = the breadth by the tongue or pointed piece of land.

Letterie. Leitir = wet hillside. I. Letteragh.

Leuchars. *Locres.* An English pl. Luachair = a rush. I. Loughermore = the great rushy place.

Leven. See Lochleven.

Lierchardele. See Leirhope.

Lillioche. Cp. the name Lylo in Armagh, and Lyiklyok in Lanark. Cp. the personal name Luloig in the Gaelic entries in the Book of Deir.

Lindifferon. *Landifferon.* Lann + dubh + fearann = church or enclosure of the dark land.

Lindoischot.

Lindores. *Londors.* Lann + dobhar = church of the water.

Lingarth. *Lingorthyn.* Linn + coirthe = pool of the pillar stones.

Lingo.

Liquorstone, near Falkland = Leckerstone, *q.v.*

Liscoureviot ("alias Lochend"). Luscar + abhaicht = cave of the dwarf.

Lizziewells. *Latishoill, Lawteishoill.* The first part "Lawteis" is a man's name, and "hoill" indicates land situated in a hollow.

Lochfitty. Loch of the Fitty Burn. Lochs took their names from the river which drained them. The name is derived from feith = a stream flowing through a marsh.

Lochgelly. *Lochgilly.* Loch + gile = loch of brightness. I. Loughgilly.

Lochleven. Leamhan = elm tree. I. Laune.

Lochmalony. *Lochualony.* Loch + lon = loch of the blackbird.

Lochore. Loch of the R. Ore, *Oir, Oar.* The Gaelic term for cold is uar or fuar, but the radical idea of fuar is water, as the derivative, fuaran = fountain, shows. The representatives of this root are Sansk. vári = water; Zend. vairi = sea, vairga = canal; Gr. οὐρία = a water-bird; Lat. urina; Norse ver, and O. E. vär = sea; Norse ûr = rain. Ore thus simply means water. Oir and ocr were Brythonic forms of Goidelic uar.

Lochornie. Loch + cornach = loch by the barley land. I. Loughorne, Loughourna.

Loch Roaddaill.

Lochran. See Drumlochtirnoch.

Lochty. This is the name of a mountain stream rising

in Benarty Hill and flowing east by Kinglassie. Before drainage, this stream formed a series of lochs and morasses, as the obsolete names Monlochty, Boglochty, and Polnavere prove, and Bogside farm is still a reminiscence. Hence Lochty was named from its forming so many watery hollows.

Logie. Lug = hollow. Anc. Logymurtache, *i.e.* Murdoch's Logie. So Murdocairnie in the same district.

Lomond Hills. This name represents a different formation from the same root as appears in Lochleven, leamhan = elm tree. In the west of Scotland in the same way the group occurs, Ben Lomond, Lochlomond, and the river Leven.

Lossley Burn.

Lothries.

Lucheld. *Leuchall, Leuchill, Loquhell.* The forms Luchall, Leuquhell, occur in Aberdeen. Leamh + coille = elm wood. See Lahill. In Ireland the name is corrupted in one instance into Longfield, the usual forms being Laughil, Loghill, and Loughill. The name Luchald exists at Dalmeny also.

Ludgeden. This name is unknown now, but the latter part, -geden, suggests strongly the old Irish name for the Firth of Forth, the sea of Giudan (Reeve's *Culdees*, p. 124), and the city in the middle of it called by Baeda Urbs Giudi.

Lumbenny. *Lumbennane.* Lom + beinnin = bare little hill.

Lumphinnans. Lann + Finan = church of St. Finan.

Lumquhat. Linn + cat = pool of the wild cats.

Lun. Linn = pool.

Lundin. *Londie.* Linn + dun = fort of the pool, the same name as London.

Lurg. Lurga = shin. I. Lurgan.

Lurgyhury.

Luscar. Luscar = cave. I. Lusgarboy.

Luthrie. Luaithre = ashes, indicating probably land where grass or heather was set on fire for agricultural improvement.

Lydox.

Lykyrstyne. This name occurs in the first entry in the Chartulary of St. Andrews in connection with the lands of Findauchty, and is described as "acervus lapidum." The name is unknown there now, but on a map of Findatie, dated 1760, one of the parks is designated Leckerston, clearly the site of the ancient Lykyrstyne. See Leckerstone.

Lynn. Linn = pool.

Machling. Mach + linn = field of the pool. Cp. Mauchline.

Madincastell = Castle of Maidens. There are ruins near Kennoway bearing this name. The Castle of Maidens of the Arthurian legends suggests that here we have another instance of Celtic myths repeating themselves in various localities. It is noteworthy that the Fife locality is situated on the lands of Dunnipace, meaning fort of the charmed serpents.

Magask. *Malgask.* Maol + gasg = the bare hill of the tail. This is the origin of the name Magus Muir.

Mailing, as in Petersmailing, *i.e.* Peter's farm. A mailing is what mail or rent is paid for, and secondarily the land itself. So the term farm originally meant the dues paid for the land.

Mairsland. Land held "pro officio mauriatus" Maer = steward. See Balwearie.

Malchrethre ("in Adnechtan"). Maol + criathar = bare rock of the sieve, the meaning being that the land around was shaking, *i.e.* boggy.

Mannerless. Same as Manorleys.

Manorleys, the lea or meadow of the demesne lands. Such names as this indicate that the manorial system with copyhold tenure prevailed far more extensively in Scotland than is supposed. At Scotlandwell a piece of land is still known as the officer's acre, the officer being the steward of the manor of Scotlandwell.

Manthrilzean. There is a word drillsean, meaning a

glimmering light, and as the first part of the word is moin = bog, the name may have arisen from the light of marsh gas generated in the morass.

Markinch. *Marching.* The termination is a corruption as shown by the earlier forms. It is derived from the personal name Marcan (K). Cp. W. Merchion (W). For similar corruptions see Dalginch and Feddinch. See Pitconmark.

Markinslaw. See the preceding name.

Mawardlary, also **Macherderrly.** Maw is now represented by Mawcarse, and Ardlary by Arlary. The second form of the name Macherderrly presents the word "mach" in its exact form as still used in Celtic. From the same word are derived such names as Rotomagus, now Rouen.

Mawcarse. Mach = field. In Ireland also the word appears as Maw amongst other forms.

Mawcloych. Mach + clach = field of the stones. This name, now obsolete, occurs in (R) alongside names in the neighbourhood of Mawcarse. In this district there are still three large pillar stones known as the Standing Stones of Orwell, and Mawcloych refers doubtless to them. From such a name having been given by Celts, the argument is strong that these stones were erected by a pre-Celtic race.

Mawcuich ("vulgo Mawhill," and now Mawhill) = field by the river Quiech. Cp. Dalquiech.

May, Isle of. Cp. Kirkmay.

Melgum. Maol + con = bare hill of the dogs.

Menegre.

Menywick.

Methil. *Methkill.* Miath + coille = soft wood. Macthail in Ireland indicates wet, soft land, and gives name to the parish of Mothel in Waterford.

Middens, The (rocks off May Isle) = The Maidens. Cp. The Maidens off the coast of Antrim.

Milnathort. *Milnquorth, Myln de Quhort.* The popular pronunciation is Mills-i-forth, just as Blairathort is found written Blairforth, and still so pronounced. A frequent corruption of the sound ch is into f (*e.g.* English laugh). Hence Milnquorth is the original form, maol + coirthe = bare hill of the standing stones.

Minzion.

Moithill, Motehill, Muithill, Muthill (of Cupar). This name is of Teutonic origin, indicating the place of the mote or meeting of the people. Muthill, in Perthshire, however, is of Celtic origin.

Moncotymire, Moncutyemyre. Moin + ciad = bog by the wood. See Coates.

Monedy. Moin + aodann = bog of the hill brow.

Moneloccodhan. This obsolete name occurs in (A) as being in Portmoak. Moin + loch + cadhan = bog of the loch of the ducks. Duck-shooting to this day is a favourite sport in the locality.

Moneyreadywell. Muine + ruadh = red shrubbery.

Monimail. *Monymele.* Muine + mil = shrubbery of honey. I. Clonmel.

Monlochty (A). Moin + Lochty = bog of the Lochty, the stream flowing east from Benarty Hill towards Kinglassie. See Lochty.

Montagart. Moin + sagart = bog of the priest. This place is described as the ecclesiastical lands of Monimail.

Montgwn. Moin + con = bog of dogs.

Montrave. *Montraive, Monthryvie.* This name is probably of the same origin as the Irish Moneenreave, or little bog of sulphur, indicating that a sulphur scum rose on the surface of the water. In the Irish name a diminutive form of moin is used. The term for sulphur is ruibh.

Montroy. Moin + ruadh = red bog.

Monturpie. Moin + Tarpaigh = Tarpy's bog. The Irish family name O'Tarpaigh, Anglicised Torpy and Tarpy, is derived from this personal name.

Monybard. Muine + bard = poets' shrubbery.

Moonzie. Muing = long, sedgy grass.

Moreland. *Morlet.* Mor + leathad = great, hill side.

Morendy.

Mossmarron. Mossmorven = moss of the big hill.

Motray. *Multray* (S). Molt, pl. muilt = wether.

Mountcoy.

Mountfleurie. *Monfloure.*

Mountquhanie. *Monquhannie.* Moin + Cainnech = Cainnech's bog. Cainnech was a well-known Irish saint, and known in Scotland as Kenneth. Kilkenny is named after him. ".Achadhbo was his principal church, and there is an abbey of his at Cill-righmonadh [St. Andrews] in Alba," *Mart. Don.*, p. 271. Kennoway church was dedicated to him. See Pitkinnie and Ramornie.

Mountquhy.

Mournipea. This seems to contain the name of Mouren, daughter of King Hungus ; a church was dedicated to her at St. Andrews (K).

Muckieloch. Muclach = piggery. I. Mucklagh.

Mugdrum. Muc + drum = boars' ridge.

Muircambus. *Morkambus, Murecambois.* Mor + camus = big, bay, or bend.

Muirmealing. See Mailing.

Munbuche. Moin + bac = bog by the bend.

Munfariyn.

Munshock Moss. Moin + scabhac = hawks' bog. I. Carrickshock.

Nakedfield. *Tornaikitaris alias Naikitfield.* Cnoc + tarbh = bull's hill. I. Knockatarry.

Naughton. *Athnauthan.* Ath + Nechtan = ford of Nechtan, whence the name MacNaughton.

Navitie. *Nevody, Nevathy, Navittie.* This name occurs also in Cromarty, and has an early spelling Nevatye. O'Reilly gives an Irish adjective neimheach, meaning glittering or shining, and Skene derives from it the word Namet or Navit, an epithet of Vipoig, a king of the Picts. I take it to belong to the same root as Old Irish nem, meaning heaven, modern Gaelic neamh, all connected with Lat. nubes, Gr. νέφος, signifying a cloud, while in Slavonic again nebo means heaven.

From Gaelic neamh comes naomh a saint, and the past participle naomhaichte, consecrated, would exactly produce such a form as Nevatye. The lands of Kirklands are conterminous with Navitie, and neimhidh in Irish signifies glebeland. The lands of Navity in Cromarty were connected with the Church, as a chaplainry was endowed from it. Still, without further corroboration of this view, it is to be assumed that the name is of an earlier origin. If the Celtic etymon for bright, referred to for the explanation of the first part of the word, is retained, the latter part may well be athan, meaning ford, so that the name would be white or bright ford. Now, in the Chartulary of St. Andrews mention is made of " the stanry furde of Nevathy," referring to Navitie in Fife, and it is only one or two generations ago since this ford was replaced by a bridge. Again, Navity in Cromarty is close to Eathie or Ethie and the Ethie burn. Cromarty itself may be from the same word. The second " r " in the name is inorganic, being introduced through sympathy with the first " r," and older forms are *Crombathy*, *Crumbauchtyn*, *Crommaty*, so that the name would mean crooked ford. See Inverdovat, where -dovat = blackford.

Neuethin. Cp. Neveth, old name of Rosneath, also the personal name Nefydd in (K).

Newark. Newwork = new building or fortification. It is described as " fortalicium de St. Monans."

Newburn. *Nithbren.* The same change is seen in the name of the river Nith in Dumfries, which is Novios in Ptolemy's Geography. Becoming Newydd = new in Brythonic, it passed into Nith under Goidelic influence. The name is allied to that of the tribe Niduari.

Nickery. Contraction of coinicer = rabbit warren, as in Irish, Nicker and Nickeres.

Nivingston. The town of the Nivens : Niven itself is a Celtic name (Mac)Cnaimhin, (Mac)Niven.

Nochnarie. See Knocknary.

Nydie. *Arnydie.* Ard + Nidan = Nidan's height. Nidan

was a Welsh saint, and Llanidan in Anglesey was
dedicated to him. He is also known in Aberdeen-
shire.

Ode Land.

Officer's Acre, The. See under Manorleys.

Ore, The (river). *Oir, Oar.* See Lochore.

Orkie. See under Denork.

Orkvenay. See under Denork.

Ormiston. Orme's town. Orme is a Scandinavian name,
as in the names Ormesby, Orme's Head, etc. See
Pittormie.

Orrock. See under Denork.

Orwell. *Orrowall, Urwell, Vuerquhell.* Iubhar + coille
= yew wood. Cp. Ury in the same district.

Otterston. Ottar's town. Ottar is a Scandinavian
name. Cp. Pittottar, just as there occur Ormiston
and Pittormie.

Outh. Uchd = the breast. I. Oughtymore.

Ovenstone. Evinstoune = Ewan's town.

Oyglethe. Og + leathad = an expanse for young animals.
Og, literally young, is said to be the origin of the term
hogg as applied to sheep.

Palgrown.

Paphle, The (of Cleish). See Pofile.

Parbroath. *Parbroith.* The first part of this name is
barr = top; for the latter part cp. the old Irish family
name O'Broith. It must be noted that very frequently
in Celtic a chief or a tribe gives name to the district
occupied.

Pardusin. This appears to be the same place as Perdew
(*q.v.*), from the descriptions given in charters.

Paris.

Paris Bridge.

Parnwell. Barr + coille = top of the wood.

Paskarmylne.

Pathcondie. *Pitcontie.* The portion of Contan. The

same name occurs between Perth and Kinross, and is corrupted into Path of Condie.

Pathemuir. Pette + mara = portion by the sea.

Perdew (and in the pl. Perdewis) alias Brumhill (D). Barr + dubh = dark top. The other name seems to be the origin of Broomhall, the seat of the Earl of Elgin.

Petcalder. Pette + coille + dobhar = portion of the wood by the water.

Petclery. Pette + cleireach = portion of the clergy.

Petculan. The portion of Culen.

Pethnathrene. Pette + trian = portion belonging to the strong man.

Petsporgin. Sporgin is probably a man's name.

Pettacherache. Pette + caorach = portion of the sheep. I. Ballynageeragh.

Pettinhaglis. Pette + eaglais = portion of the Church.

Pettultin. Pette + Ultan = portion of Ultan. The name Ultan appears in the *Liber Hymnorum* as author of a hymn in praise of Brigit. He is described as belonging to Dal Conchobair, that is, to the tribe of Connor, and Connor is found in Fife in the name Balgonar.

Pettuscall. A similar name occurs in the Chartulary of Brechin in the forms Pettintoscall, Pettintoskell. This represents exactly the pronunciation of Pette an t-soisgeul = portion of the Gospel. Pettuscall is described as "terræ ecclesiasticæ." Cp. Bantuscall.

Phantassie. Fan + tais = damp slope. See Teasses.

Pickletillum. This is a greater corruption than the form assumed by the same name in Aberdeen, Pictillum. Pette + talamh = portion of fine land.

Pilcolm. Pill + colum = river inlet of the pigeons.

Pilkembare. Pill + cam + bar = river inlet of the crooked summit.

Pillow, The.

Pilmuir. Pill + mara = river inlet of the sea.

Pirniss. An English pl. Of the same origin as Barns, *q.v.*

Pitbauchlie. *Petbaclachin.* Pette + bachlag = portion of the shoots or blades of grass.

Pitbladdo. *Pitbladar.* See under Bladdershaw.

Pitbrog. Pette + brog = portion of the shoe. This must have been the shoemaker's allotment. See Runbroig.

Pitbullieslak (S).

Pitcairlie. Petcarlingis = portion of the carlings. (R) is the authority for Petcarlingis; it is to be noted, however, that (MS) gives the names Pittuncarley and Pitcarlie as distinct places but in the same district.

Pitcairn. Portion abounding in cairns.

Pitconmark. *Petconmarchin.* Portion of Conmark. The name Marcan gives Markinch, so with the common Celtic name prefix Con- we get Conmark, cp. Cinmarc (K), Cynvarch (W). The name Petmarch also existed in Fife.

Pitconnoquhy. The portion of [Mac] Conochie (= Duncanson).

Pitcorthie. *Pettecorthin.* Pette + coirthe = portion of the pillar stones. Cp. Balgallin, Rumgally, Mawcloych. The Ordnance Survey shows standing stones at all the Fife Pitcorthies.

Pitcullo. *Pitculloze, Pitculloche.* The portion of [Mac] Culloch.

Pitdinnie. Pette + dion = portion of the place of shelter.

Piteadie. Pette + Aedan = Aedan's portion.

Pitfar. Pette + fear = portion of the men.

Pitfechies. Pette + fitheach = portion of the ravens.

Pitfirrane. *Petfurane.* Pette + fuaran = portion of the spring or fountain.

Pitgorno. *Pitgornach.* Garnach's (K) portion.

Pitkeavy. Pette + ciabhach = the portion producing marshy grass. I. Keevagh.

Pitkeirie. Pette + Ciarraidhe, the latter portion being the tribal name whence Kerry is derived.

Pitkennetit = the portion of Kennedy.

Pitkinnie. *Pitkanye.* Cainnech's, i.e. Kenneth's portion.

Pitlair. Pette + lar = middle portion.

Pitlessie.   Pette + lios = portion abounding in good garden ground.

Pitlethie.   *Pitlathie.*   Pette + Liathan = Liathan's portion.

Pitliver.   Cp. Liverpool and the Welsh name Llywernog. It may be cognate with Lat. *lupus*, and so Pitliver would be portion abounding in wolves.

Pitlochie.   Portion near the loch.

Pitlour.   *Petenlouir.*   Pette + lobhar = portion of the lepers.

Pitlumbertie.   Pette + lann + Brigit = portion of church of St. Bride.

Pitmedden.   Pette + meadhon = middle portion.

Pitmenzies.   *Pitmunzies.*   Pette + muing = sedgy portion.

Pitmiclardie.   M'Clarty's portion.

Pitmilly.   *Petmulin.*   Pette + muilleann = portion of the mill.

Pitmossie.

Pitnaurcha.   Cp. the name Bridge of Orchy, and see Orkie.

Pitreavie.   Pette + riabhach = gray or brindled portion. It refers to the variegated strips of different crops grown.   I. Gortrevagh.

Pitscottie.   Pette + sgothach = flowery portion.

Pitsoulie.   The latter part seems to be identical with the personal name Soulis.   It is probably of Teutonic origin.   Cp. the name Soulisby and perhaps Selby.

Pittarthie.   Portion of Art or Arthur.

Pittarvie.   Pette + tarbh = portion of bulls.

Pittauchop.

Pittencrieff.   Pette + craobh = portion of the trees.

Pittendriech.   Pette + fraoch = heathery portion.

Pitteuchar.   *Petioker.*   Pette + ucaire = fuller's portion.

Pittiloch.   *Petedache.*   Pette + clach = portion of the stones.

Pittinhaggilis.   Pette + eaglais = portion of the Church.

Pittormie.   Pette + Orme = Orme's portion.   Cp. Ormiston.

Pittottar.   Pette + Ottar = Ottar's portion.   Cp. Otterston.

Pittowie.   Pette + dubhan = portion of the dark man. Cp. the name M'Ildowie.

Pittuncarty.   *Pettoncardy.*   Pette + cearda = portion of the artificers.

Plains.

Pleasance. French, *plaisance*, maison de plaisance.

Poffle, The (of Strathkinness). Poffle signifies a small farm or pendicle. I think it is identical with bachille of the same meaning. Bachle in O. F. means a small piece of land, and the word bachelor is derived from it, that probably being the amount of land necessary for that rank on the road to knighthood.

Polduff. Poll + dubh = black pool.

Polnaber. *Polnavere.* Poll + abar = pool of the miry place. As the land is now drained the mire as well as the name has disappeared. So near it the name Monlochty has gone, that is, the bog formed by the Lochty burn.

Portmoak. *Pettenmokane.* Pette + Mochan = the portion of Mochain, a man's name in old Irish. The local pronunciation to this day is Pitmoag.

Powguild. Poll + geal = white pool.

Powmill. Poll + muileann = pool of the mill.

Prathouse. See Pratis.

Pratis. *Pratirris, Prateris.* This and the preceding name seem to be taken from the personal name Prat derived from St. Protus. See Brotus. Cp. Protstown in Banff.

Prinlaws. *Prenlas.*

Purin. *Pourane.* Poll + raith = ferny pool. I. Pollraine.

Pusk. *Pursk, Purcswich.* The last part is the Scandinavian *wick*, a village, and the first is a man's name.

Pyeston. *Pyotstoun.* Magpies' town.

Quheitquerrellhoupe = the anchorage near the white quarry.

Quiech. Cuach = hollow in a hill, hence applied to a river flowing out of the hollow.

Radernie. Rath + airne = fort of the sloe trees.

Raith. The Raithe. The "wread," or place for confining cattle in winter. See under Kiras for the origin of the term.

Rambothie. Rann + both = division of the huts.

E

Rameldry. *Rathmeldry, Ramelrike.* The latter part seems to involve a personal name, as Melric, so that the name means Melric's fort.

Ramoir. Rath + mor = great fort. I. Ramore Point at Portrush.

Ramornie. *Ramorgnie, Ramorgany.* Rath + mor + Cainnech = the great fort of Cainnech. See Mount-quhanie.

Rankeillour. Rann + coille + dobhar = the portion of the wood by the water.

Rathelpie. *Rathelpin.* Rath + Alpin = Alpin's fort.

Rathillet. *Rathalet, Rathulet.* Rath + Uladh = the fort of Ulster.

Redwalls. So called from the iron scum rising on the surface of the water. See Strathruddie.

Reelpinton.

Rescobie. Ros + Colbain = the promontory of Colbain.

Rhynd. Rinn = point or promontory.

Rimalton. Rimmel's town.

Rintoul. *Rentouill.* Rinn + toll = the point of the hollow.

Rires. *Riras, Rerays (schira de).* A comparison of this name with such names as Rywrayis, Bulwrayis in Renfrew, and Wrae or Wraith in various districts, points out as the explanation of the latter part of the name the old Scottish word Wread or Wreath, signifying a small enclosure for confining cattle or for growing crops. The "reed" is still the name in Fife for the court where cattle are enclosed in winter. The term appears in Old Norse in such words as naep-nareitr, a place for growing turnips. Rerays signifies enclosures for growing rye. The root idea is tying up or enclosing; in Gothic vrithus means a herd. See Raith.

Risk, The. This is the name of a field on an old plan of Findatic. Riasc = marsh. I. Roosky.

Rodmannan. *Rothimanand.* This place seems to have been near St. Andrews. The latter part involves the same word as appears in Clackmannan and Slamannan, for which see Skene and Rhys.

Rossyth. Ros + saighead = promontory of the arrows.

Rufflets = rough flat or meadow.

Rumdewan. Rann + Dubhan = division of Dubhan (*i.e.* the little dark man). I. Randouan.

Rumgally. *Ramgally, Ratmagallan.* Rath + gallan = fort of the pillar stones.

Runbroig ("part of Balsasny"). Rann + brog = division of the shoe. See Pitbrog. I. Knocknabrogue.

Ryelaw. *Rialie, Royallie.*

St. Monans. This saint's name is also preserved in the name Kilminning, *q.v.*

Saline. *Sauelyn.* Sabhal = a barn.

Salrais-medow. Cp. Salramedow (S) in Roxburgh. The first part of this name seems to be sal, a word in all the Teutonic languages signifying an abode or hall, and sometimes applying to a place for storing crops. The latter is wread, an enclosure (see Riras) ; so the word means an enclosure for an erection for storing crops.

Salveneich (Salveynche). This seems to be the same name as Sealvanach, son of Eogan, king of Dalriada. (K).

Sauchope. *Salchop.* Perhaps the hope or bay by the saugh or willow trees.

Scabert.

Scololand. Scoloes (Pictish scolofthes, explained by Latin scholasticus) seem to have been originally the lowest order of clergy, and employed in agriculture, and subsequently to have become simply the term for the small tenants under the clergy. Thus there were "scologlands" in Ellon and in Arbuthnot held under St. Andrews. The name scolog in Ireland means a small farmer, as in the name Scullogestoun.

Scoonie. *Sconin.*

Scotlandwell. "Fons Scotiae." It does not appear when this name was given. It became titular of one of the few religious houses in Scotland termed a ministry, this foundation being lord of the manor of Scotlandwell. The Church was probably the giver of the name, as it superseded sometimes earlier names, *e.g.* Kirkness and Spittle.

Scotstarvet. This means Tarvet owned by a Scott. It seems to have been previously called Inglistarvet, as being owned by an Inglis.

Seggie. *Sagy.* Cp. the ancient river name Segeia, supposed to be the Mersey, and the tribal name Segantii.

Serisland. *Siresland, Scheirisland, Scheires.* See Ceres.

Shambleton. Sean + baile = old town. Cp. Shambellie in Dumfries.

Shanwell. Sean + baile = old town.

Sheardrum. Siar + drum = western ridge.

Shirend. " Shire " here probably means barony, and the name indicates the most distant point of a barony.

Shiresbare.

Shires Mill. There were many " shires " in Fife, and the word seems to have been equivalent to barony, so that Shires Mill indicates the barony mill.

Shirram Brae.

Shoolbraids. Scumhal + braghad = steep hill of the gorge. I. For the first part of the name Shoolbraids, Drumscool, and for the second the Braid in Antrim. So in Scotland the Braid Hills near Edinburgh, and Breadalbane.

Sillerhole. A place about which there must have been a legend to the effect that there was treasure there.

Sillock. Saileach = willow. I. Silloge.

Silverbarton. Barton belonging to one of the name of Sölvar.

Silverburn. See Sillerhole.

Silverton. See Silverbarton.

Sisterislandis. This refers to a custom where land was divided among all the children, but a daughter's share was less than that of a son. Cp. the term sister-part in Shetland.

Skaildowhillis. Sgail + dubh = dark shade.

Skeddoway. *Scathochy.* Scothach = flowery place.

Skelpie. Scealp = cleft or chasm.

Skilmervie. Sgail + mor + beinn = shadow of the big hill.

Skryne. From Latin scrinium = shrine. I. Skrine.

Slungie Hill. Sliabh + Angus = hill of Angus.

Solsgirth. Perhaps identical with the old name Saltgirs.

Sorbie.

Soytourlandis. A suitor was one who held land under a tenure which obliged him to appear in Court on behalf of his superior.

Spalefield. See Spawell.

Spale Inn. See Spawell.

Spawell. A well for telling fortunes; the same word appears in spaewife. The word is etymologically equivalent to Lat. specio.

Spittal = Hospital. Cp. Dalnaspidal. Spittle is a very common name in Ireland.

Standalane.

Stankhill. Stank is an old Sc. word for an open ditch for draining land.

Star. Sturr = pointed rock.

Starley Burn. Sturr + liath = gray pointed rock.

Starrlaw. See preceding.

Steelend. This name indicates a place for putting up horses, being cognate with stall.

Stenhouse.

Stenton. *The Stentoune.*

Stovie. Stove in old Sc. means vapour or mist, so Stovie is a dewy place.

"With hailsum stouis ouerheildand the slak."—DOUG., *Virgil.*

Strabo Muir. Strath + bo = cows' strath. It is described as "communis pastura."

Strathairly. Strath + ard + liath = strath of the gray height.

Strathendry. *Strathanery.* Strath + righ = king's strath.

Strathkinness. Strath of the Kinness Burn. Kinness appears also in the form Kineth. If this is correct, the meaning is Kenneth's Burn.

Strathmiglo. *Strathmigloche.* The strath of the Miglo stream. See Craigmiglo.

Strathruddie. Strath + ruide = strath of the red iron scum. The iron from the soil appears on the surface of the water, giving it a *reddish* colour. I. Raruddy.

Strathtyrum. Strath + tioram = the dry strath.

Stravithy. Strath + beith = strath of the birch trees.

Stronachy Hill. Sron = the nose. The letter "t" is frequently inserted between *s* and *r*.

Sunnyside. Lands were on division distinguished by the terms sunny half and shady half.

Sypsies. To "sipe" is to ooze, and sypsies must mean land kept wet with a number of small springs. Cp. Sypland in Galloway.

Sythrum. *Shyrthrum* (?). Siar + drum = western ridge. The name appears as Sheardrum in Saline.

Swallowdrum.

Swilken Burn, The.

Swinky. *Swinccowhill.*

Tailabout. Cp. the Fife name Cuffabout.

Tarbet. East and West (Isle of May). These are the names at the two extremities of a narrow neck of land in the Isle of May. The name is more accurately Tarbert, and is used both in Scotland and in Ireland to indicate a narrow isthmus across which boats could be carried from sea to sea. Cp. E. and W. Tarbert in Kintyre, Tarbet in Loch Lomond, Tarbert in Harris, and Tarbert in Ireland.

Tarhill. Tor = hill.

Tarvet. *Tarbat.* This name is of the same origin as Tarbet, *q.v.*

Teasses. *Taisses.* An English pl. Tais = moist or damp. Cp. Hantassyn near Islay.

Tents Moor. An English pl. of teinte pl. of teine = fire. I. Tents.

Tethyknowe.

Teuchat. *Tuquhitesse.* Tigh + Cait = house of Cait.

Thainislandis. The lands of a thane. The term thane

was preserved in Scotland much later than England, and designated a tenant of lands under the crown. Cp. such names as Thainstoun in Aberdeen and in Kincardine, and Thaynisnett in Banff.

Thimblehill. Perhaps named like Thimbletown in Ireland, the flowers of the foxglove being referred to.

Thirlstone. This means a stone drilled or bored for some purpose, just as the Bore Stone at Bannockburn where Bruce's standard was fixed.

Thomanean. *Tomenaygne.* Tom + eun = hill of birds. This is another instance of the old spelling trying to approximate the Celtic pronunciation.

Thornton. This may be identical with the old name Thoriston.

Thre.

Threapmuir. From the old Sc. word threip, meaning to quarrel or debate. The name may commemorate the site of a controversy either as to the ownership of the land or of some other matter of dispute in the district. Many Irish names arise from the same circumstance, *e.g.* Quintinmanus. A similar state of affairs made Horace say of himself, "Lucanus an Apulus anceps."

Tichindod, or, as it is usually written, Dichindod. The first part is tech = house.

Tillybreck. Tulach + breac = speckled hill.

Tillyochie. Tulach = hill.

Tillyrie. Tulach + reidh = hill in the plain.

Tillywhally. Tulach + coille = hill of the wood.

Tippermacoy. Tiobar + MacAodha = Mackay's well.

Tippermure. Tiobar + mor = great well.

Tipperton. See preceding entry.

Tolibrench.

Tolybotheville.

Tongueis. Ton + giumhas = back of the firs.

Topitlaw. Topit is the same name as the Irish hill of Topped applied to a round hill. The Gaelic adjective is topach = having a tuft or crest, and is identical with the English word top. Cp. the expression "a weel-tappit hen."

Torbain.   Tor + ban = white hill.

Torloisk.   Tor + loisgthe = hill of burning (*i.e.* of the heather).

Torr.   This name probably indicates here a tower-like hill. The word, however, seems to have its proper meaning of an artificial tower in such old Fife names as Torcatholach, Torforret, and Tornacataris.

Tosh.

Touchie.   *Techyntulchy, Thentulchy.*   Tech + tulach = house on the hill.

Transylaw.   For Tansylaw.   Tansy is a tall plant with small yellow flowers.   O. F. tanasic.

Trapinthie.

Travalay.   See Dovolay.   The first part of the name seems to be the common Brythonic word tref, meaning a dwelling.

Treaton.   *Tratone, Trettoun, Trittoun.*

Trolbanyre or **Tarvane,** perhaps the same place as Turlvany.

Troustrie.   Trostry.   Cp. Troustir in Cowal and Trostane in Carrick.   Named after St. Drostan, who is described in connection with Markinch as Modrustus, *mo* = my, being often prefixed to saints' names in Irish.

Tulliallan.   Tulach + aluinn = beautiful hill.   I. Tully-allen.

Tulliebole.   Tulach + Bacighill = the hill of Boyle.   Cp. Maybole.

Tullylumb.   Tulach + lom = bare hill.

Turfhills.   Tarbh + coille = bull's wood.

Turlvany.

Tushielaw.   Dishilago = Sc. name for the coltsfoot plant.

Tyrie.

Uneakeris, Unakeris.

Unthank.   This name occurs frequently in Scotland, and sometimes in the form Winthank.   It is derived from uinseann = ash tree.   In Ireland Unshinagh means a

place abounding in ash trees. In the South of
Scotland the name appears as Inshanks, while in
(S) Perth has Unschenach, and Lanark Uncheno.
In the South of Ireland the word has "f" prefixed, so
that the name appears as Funshinagh.

Urquhart. Urchair = a throw, or cast of an athlete.

Ury. This was the name of a streamlet running into
Lochleven south of Milnathort. It is derived from
iubhar = yew tree, and signifies a place abounding in
yews. I. Uragh, or with the article prefixed Newry.
See Orwell.

Uthrogle. *Utrogenalle, Utherogale.*

Vane, The. A'bheinn = the hill (bheinn being pronounced
approximately vane).

Vantage.

Vicarford. The vicar's ford.

Vows, The, East and West. Cp. Elanvow and Elan-
vanow in Lochlomond.

Wanleyis. Dark coloured or dirty meadows. Wan is
an old Sc. word.

Waterless. This is for water leas or meadows. Cp.
Mannerless and Bredles.

Waulkmill. The fulling mill.

Weddersbie. Wethers' town. Cp. Balmuto.

Wemyss. An English pl. of uaimh = cave.

Whorlawhill. Cor = round hill. The name seems to
comprise three words of the same meaning.

Winthank. See Unthank.

Wolmanstoun. Wolfman's town.

Wolmerstoun. Wolmer's town.

Womanhill, The ("apud Largo"). Wolfman's hill.

Wormit. *The Wormet.* Worm or Orm in Scandinavian
means a serpent. The article in Scandinavian -et is
postfixed to the noun. *The* Wormet is thus an
intelligible duplication.

OMISSA

Cellardyke.   Formerly called Skinfasthaven, or Skynfisch-
heaven.

Dalkeith.   This name of lands in Kinross-shire (formerly
in Perthshire) has been referred to for the explanation
of several names such as Inverkeithing. Dalkeith
signifies the field or district of Cait, one of the eponymous sons of Cruithne. The name Cait is involved
in Caithness as one of the seven divisions of the Picts
in Scotland. The name appears also as Got (K),
hence the Fife name Goatmilk.

THE END

www.ingramcontent.com/pod-product-compliance
Lightning Source LLC
Chambersburg PA
CBHW020253090426
42735CB00010B/1902